# OFF-GRID PROJECTS

*Tips and Tricks of Effective Survival Techniques to Survive Anywhere, Building Solar Systems for Your Daily Living and Do-It-Yourself Projects Like Rain Barrels and Chicken Coops*

# JIMSON LEWIS

# Table of Contents

# Introduction

Nowadays, many people are turning to survivalism and off-grid living. And for a good reason! From a global perspective, the array of crises we've had to endure, coupled with uncertainty about the future and a lack of prospects, are pushing more and more folks to return to some basics. In fact, who hasn't read about or seen families who decided to leave it all behind and start anew? Living minimally in wood cabins, collecting rainwater, recycling, growing fresh fruit and vegetables, and raising farm animals while relying on sustainable energy sources. How do they do it, and why? Fearing natural catastrophes or the dislocation of society and its disastrous consequences, it isn't hard to grasp why that kind of lifestyle would appeal to many progressive and well-reasoned individuals worldwide.

Living off-the-grid comes down to one central premise: Using everything nature offers to achieve a self-sufficient, sustainable, eco-responsible lifestyle. While we can very well be thankful for modern life's convenient amenities (in Western societies, at least), our collective carbon footprint and irreversible damage to the planet make us think twice about that acquired comfort. So, whether you're looking to distance yourself from increasingly toxic living environments or want to awaken to survivalists inside you for your upcoming adventure trip, going off-grind is an excellent way to challenge everything you were taught until now to experience a healthier, more gratifying life.

This book aims to introduce you to survival living and off-grid DIY projects. Page after page, you'll garner useful knowledge that will empower you and prepare you to live on the edge of modern society, away from commotion and pollution and without access to electricity, running water, or grocery stores. Even if you don't know the first thing about surviving outside your comfort zone, that's quite all right. Everything mentioned here can easily be understood by any 12-year-old with basic science knowledge. What's more, each chapter contains detailed, step-by-step tutorials on how to complete a variety of useful and rewarding projects.

To give a brief overview, we'll define what the off-grid lifestyle is, its countless benefits, and how it can bring you closer to self-sufficiency in terms of power, food, and health needs. We'll illustrate this with some popular examples of off-grid projects. Next, you'll be introduced to different types of rain barrels and how to raise chickens and build a coop. Chapters four and five are dedicated to solar and wind energy and how you can leverage those natural resources to generate power for daily living (with pros and cons and building instructions for each). We'll then move on to farming and bee farming, starting a kitchen garden, and we'll list some of the food items you can expect to grow in limited spaces. Chapter eight is all about greenhouses, how they differ from regular gardens, and how to build one. Finally, the closing chapter will provide examples of even more inspiring off-grid projects you can undertake to move one step closer to self-sufficiency and healthy personal finances.

Now, before we begin, let's get something clear: Living off the grid is not an endeavor to be pursued "for fun." You'll need to be resourceful, adaptable, fearless, and rely on your most primal instincts if your objective is to truly become self-sufficient. But with good base knowledge and plenty of drive and willpower, that goal will be well within reach.

If you're ready for this transition, by all means, let's jump right in!

# Chapter 1

# What the Off-Grid Lifestyle Is

## What It Means to Be Off-Grid

If I asked you to name human necessities, what would you think about? Food and water, of course. Now, what if I ask you to name something more? Will you say shelter? Most probably. Then, I will ask you to think about a third necessity. I'm sure you thought about services, like electricity, water, and gas.

Interesting how such valuable resources were merely third positioned in the hierarchy of needs. Although if we think about it, it is not that strange.

Surviving is based mainly on eating and drinking water, which has been that way for millions of years. Naturally, we cannot live outside at the mercy of harsh weather and wild animals. We need four walls and a roof. That leads us to the third group of needs: services.

It is a fact that humanity has managed to live without electricity and the internet for centuries, without resulting in significant losses or problems.

Do you need heat during winter? Get some logs, put them in the fireplace, light it, and the problem is solved! Are there problems with light? Do you find it impossible to see in the middle of the night? The answer is easy. Get some candles, and you can keep reading and studying.

After all, it seems that the more we reflect upon this, the more we realize services are, all in all, luxuries.

Now, you probably think I am crazy to make that statement. Yes, anyone can survive without light and running water, but that's for a primitive lifestyle. Why would we want to do that? We are no longer living in caves. We gave up on lances, bows, and arrows long ago. We are in the 21st Century and live a lifestyle that demands internet connection, electricity, and hot water. How could anyone afford to live without them?

It makes sense to see it that way. The problem is that many of these modern necessities are, in part, the cause of plenty of suffering and damage. For the planet, we can name climate change and pollution. For ourselves, passive, anxious, and depressed. This is not only a matter of being "too connected." It has to do with managing our resources, what foods we consume, and what habits we choose.

So, how can we find a balance between living a healthier lifestyle for the planet and ourselves and simultaneously not giving up on our modern basic needs?

Fortunately, there is a solution. What if I told you that it is possible to acquire those services without relying on utilities? What if, instead of polluting the air and wasting water to create energy, we rely on reusable, natural sources?

If this sounds like a dream come true, it's because it is! Also, it's not just a once-off thing. Rather, it is a lifestyle: the off-grid lifestyle.

When living off-grid, we don't depend on public or private utilities. Instead, energy is gathered from renewable sources. For instance, the wind and sun are sources of infinite power and sufficient to generate free electricity.

Moreover, living off-grid has an array of advantages. You can reunite with your roots and become self-sufficient while protecting the planet and reducing pollution in all forms. If you have ever wanted to be fully independent, this is what you were looking for.

Welcome to the off-grid lifestyle.

Why you are choosing independence with the off-grid lifestyle

A free-spirited life can be attainable by going off the grid. Being unrestrained is probably the main reason people switch to this style. But how can it grant freedom?

First, you find freedom in not relying on others for energy. Secondly, it provides a chance to choose where you want to live. All in all, it makes you a more self-sustainable person. Considering that living off-the-grid is strictly related to living in a natural environment, it is no surprise to find many creating their own home.

To live off the grid, you must choose the proper region and the elements to build the house. Of course, this can be an opportunity to design your home according to your taste and convenience.

What's more, even if you don't start a house from scratch, there's still plenty of freedom in the off-grid world. Many decide to buy their houses far from urban areas and fully develop off-grid activities. Another thing relating to freedom is the financial aspect behind this lifestyle.

There is no denying that the very first approach will demand some investment. However, it will pay off in the future. Going off-grid is a long-term investment. Instead of paying electric bills every month, you can once put money into solar panels and batteries. Give it some time to gain the panel's investment back. You'll be surprised how much you can save by not paying bills.

There are more fields in which you won't be wasting money anymore. Living off-grid means you'll be sowing and harvesting your fruit and vegetables, which provides seeds for future crops. It is a non-stop system, which ultimately cuts costs. But, please, let's not think solely about capital. The benefits of growing your food are plenty and more quality-oriented.

For example, organic vegetables are free of pesticides or any other artificial additive, leading to healthier food, and your body will be forever grateful.

Besides, the more you eat a healthy diet, the further you keep from fast food. You'll wish you started earlier when you feel the results:

boosted immunity, lower heart diseases, and a longer life expectancy. It will be like living inside a brand new body.

All in all, an off-the-grid style can do wonders for your body. But, if you think it's merely related to farm food, you are wrong. That is just the tip of the iceberg.

Living off-grid means you'll be experiencing more outdoor activities. For instance, you decide to build a home yourself. That task will demand lots of hard work, digging, and lifting. However, even if you buy an already constructed house, being off-grid forces you to stay in touch with nature. It won't be a surprise if you start jogging, hiking, or taking long walks to spend your free time. Compare them to the activities the majority living in urban environments are used to. They watch an entire series in days, mindlessly scroll through social media, or play video games for hours. All these forms of entertainment are fun, but the more you indulge in them, the lazier you become. Eventually, you find it is harder to get out of bed and face the day. Now, doing the complete opposite will guarantee opposite results. For many, an off-the-grid life forces them to reduce media consumption and other forms of distractions. With so much free time, the only alternative will be to get out of the house and explore the surroundings.

Another plus is that this behavior will grant better sleep. A good rest also boosts your immune system and mood, improves your memory, prevents weight gain, and drastically lowers heart diseases.

Lastly, constant contact with the environment provides fresher air for your lungs, and a good amount of oxygen also strengthens the immune system.

Now that I mentioned health, let's point out the importance of medicine in off-grid activities. The relevance of medical health systems cannot be denied. What cannot be denied either is the many ways in which nature gifted humanity with homemade solutions to common disorders. Headaches, inflammations, irritations, and flu can all be treated with plants and derivatives. Growing them in your garden is a cheap investment and will be another saving.

It is fascinating to reflect upon this. Moving to an off-grid home improves your health significantly in various ways: better food, better sleep, better body, better humor, and better habits. But, having so much to choose from, where should you start?

## You Don't Have to Live Off-Grid to Do Off-Grid

Up to this section, there are only two options you are thinking about:

The first is that you are already packing your clothes and saying goodbye to the suburbs. Off-the-grid life is too good to ignore.

The other option is that you have become repulsed by so much wilderness. Why would you give up the comforts of civilization to dive into nothingness, get dirty all the time, and cut wood every day to heat your house?

Sure. It is understandable. Going from one extreme to the other seems scary and an impossible task. However, before you stop reading, give me another chance. You will like what's about to come. You may not want to live completely off-grid, but you can add off-grid activities to your way of living.

In other words, there are lots of off-grid projects you can implement without getting rid of your T.V., computer, and Nintendo Switch. You don't even need to move to carry them out. For instance, no one stops you from cultivating your vegetables. If you have a garden, take some days off and create a vegetable plot. You don't need to discard supermarket food completely. You have to add two or three self-harvested fresh greens to your diet. You'll realize how good they taste, and they save you money in the long run. You will feel better eating healthier, but you will also feel proud of producing your food.

Additionally, you can switch from one power source to another. More specifically, you can acquire solar panels and install them in your house. Of course, you'll need to invest some money in it. But, as I previously mentioned, ultimately, in the long run, this saves more than what you spent initially. Did I mention that you'll be saving the environment too? Solar panels are eco-friendly because there is no greenhouse gas emission. Their energy is clean and renewable.

As you have seen, an off-grid life can be achieved by anyone. After all, you select the options that suit your interest and capacities. Maybe, getting a solar panel seems too much, but planting vegetables is an easy job if you have a backyard. Or maybe installing a greywater system turns out to be a fun task. Who knows?

You have to start with the ones you think will improve your life. Then, you can move to the rest. Give a chance to only one; you and your loved ones won't regret it.

## Aspects That Make a Project Off-Grid

An off-the-grid project can be anything that works independently from public services. It is a project designed autonomously, not relying on external sources.

Off-grid projects can be individual or communal. It is common to find large groups of families living together, sharing the same areas. Communal living creates a sense of community and belonging, in which every part benefits from one another's activities. Essentially, more people can do more tasks, and sharing the investments makes for more economical spending.

However, it's common that many prefer living off-grid on their own or with their partner. It means that thorough preparation should be taken beforehand, and every detail is considered.

Whether one form or the other, the off-the-grid lifestyle is a possibility.

**Off-Grid Activities and Why They Matter**

Below you'll find some off-grid activities. If you want to start an off-the-grid life, these will help you decide which ones will be a priority. If not, they will come in handy in choosing the activities you want to implement in your daily life.

*The Solar Power Systems*

The sun is an infinite fountain of power. Solar energy is gathered and transformed into electricity. There are two forms in which this occurs. The first one is through photovoltaic (PV) panels. PV panels are various individual cells, when connected, create electricity. The other option is a solar mirror. These mirrors reflect and focus solar radiation toward receivers that gather energy. Ultimately, this produces heat. Both PV panels and solar-thermal mirrors complement each other. After all, the heat collected from the mirrors can also produce electricity.

Once the energy is gathered, it can be stored in thermal storage or batteries for future use. A pivotal aspect of these elements is that the solar power systems also function as water heaters. Ultimately, solar panels allow us to eliminate two costly services: heat and electricity.

Bear in mind that these cannot be placed by yourself like a DIY project. You need an expert to install them. However, once it is done, it will provide unlimited energy.

One last relevant detail to consider. If you plan to install solar panels, installing a backup power supply is recommended, too. A secondary power source is very convenient on cloudy days or if unexpected technical issues emerge with the panels. Some of these backup alternatives could be a wind or hydropower turbine.

### *The Wind System*

A small wind electric system can work together with a solar electric component. As a result, you have a hybrid power system. Before implementing this, the aspects to consider are living in a zone where annual wind speed reaches nine miles per hour and the capacity to install the system in the area.

Overall, it is a better option to rely on solar power systems. However, considering this alternative is not a bad idea, especially if you can rely on both.

### *Water Well and Other Forms of Gathering Water*

You can get water from other sources, not necessarily a private or public service. Digging a well for water can be done by yourself or by professionals.

Once again, paying for a water well is not a low-budget investment. Nonetheless, you'll be grateful for the results once the payment is made. Remember, a solar power system serves for heating water, too. Installing a well and a solar panel kills two birds with one stone.

Of course, there may be some doubts regarding the pollution of the water. Is it safe to make a homemade well? It is! If the hole is deep enough, the water you take out will be cleaner. If your doubts are still persistent, always remember that you can filter or boil the water before drinking it, but what if you consider digging a well too much effort? What are the alternatives?

The most obvious answer is to gather water from a river or lake. Living near these natural sources will provide perpetual liquid for washing or drinking. This option is only available for places where lakes and rivers are nearby. While this is not possible for everyone, there is still a better choice found everywhere: rain.

Gathering rainwater is demanding. Actually, collecting the water is not the problem. The hard part is cleaning it. But ultimately, it is yet another form of freedom. Storing rainwater can be done by placing barrels, buckets, and tanks along with your surroundings. If you don't want to consume that water, at least it serves for washing clothes or dishes. It can equally work for flushing your toilet or gardening.

However, there is yet another form of using water for the toilet and the crops. It is not a must, but it will pay off if you can afford it. I'm talking about the greywater system. This setup recycles wastewater used for cooking, cleaning, and washing. Naturally, this water cannot be drunk but is perfect for flushing and fertilization. Remember, mismanaging water usage negatively impacts the environment. Reusing bath and kitchen water is an excellent and economical way of taking care of the Earth.

### *The Septic Tank System*

Clean water is a must. However, you should have a plan of what to do with the dirty water. I'm saying that one inevitably will need to get rid of wastewater. More precisely, toilet water. Sewage cannot be thrown away anywhere, and it would pollute the environment. Of course, it would be utterly disgusting. The best option is to build a homemade septic tank system. Every waste will be accumulated in the watertight chamber. From there, two routes are met depending on the material. Solids stay in the chamber until a septic truck arrives and vacuums all the waste away. Regarding liquids, those moving to a septic drain field.

Sure enough, installing this system demands more money and time yet. Luckily, there is an alternative that comes with a benefit. Instead of setting a watertight chamber, you can purchase a compost toilet. Believe it or not, human waste also functions as a fertilizer. In other words, you can empty the compost toilet in the garden for stronger crops.

## *Avoid Using Too Many Electric Devices*

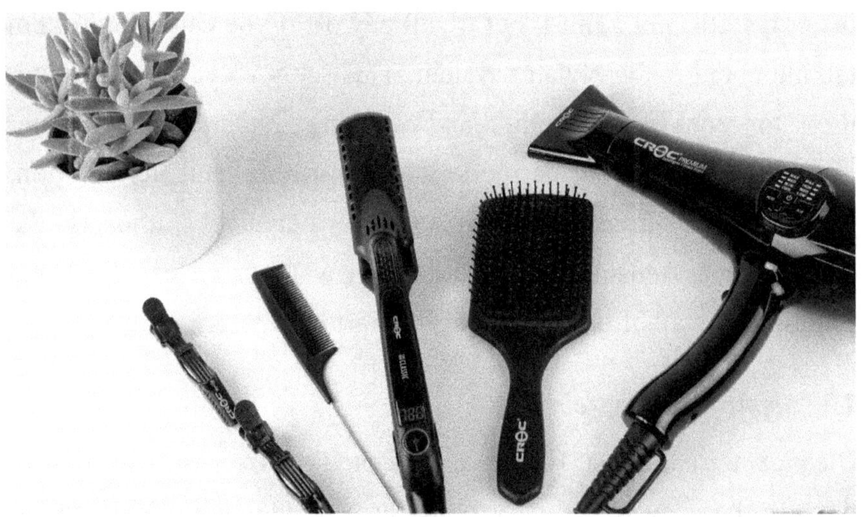

There are so many objects and devices we can live without. One example is the hairdryer. Why use it when you can dry your hair with a towel and the air? The same logic applies to other electronic devices, including toasters, electric razors, microwaves, electric grills, and everything you believe can be done without electricity. Trust me. The alternatives are out there. It's a matter of using your imagination.

## *Reducing Trash*

Lowering the number of waste you produce is not only an off-grid activity. It is something that should and could be done by everyone. The thing is, living off-grid demands reducing your garbage. Living off-grid means most people cannot rely on trash pick-up services. In this scenario, the wisest decision is to produce the least amount of waste materials. However, reducing garbage is only one side of the coin. The other aspect that goes hand in hand is recycling. Recycling forces the reuse of cans and disposable pots for food storage. It makes a person think twice before buying non-reusable packages. It encourages people to move from plastic to glass and use banana or potato peels for gardening.

### *Growing, Gathering, and Hunting Your Food*

A lot of reasons make growing your food a top-notch option. You save money, eat healthier, and the food is fresher and more delicious. Vegetables will be pesticide-free and beneficial for the environment.

Another detail that seems to be forgotten when talking about harvesting is the joy behind the activity. All in all, it is a vigorous outdoor exercise that comes with a rewarding sense of pride. Plus, after so much work, you'll be grateful and appreciate your food even more.

Now, let's talk about "looking for" your food. For instance, if you move to live in the forests, you might find trees that grow fruits, berries, and nuts. You could also find mushrooms on the floor, but you must know they are not poisonous. The thrill of the hunt is also a fulfilling experience. It's a way of pushing yourself to learn about the place you live in.

Moreover, now that we mentioned the hunt, you might be interested in turning it into a food supplement. Some places are the homes of many wild animals that you could hunt. If the area has a lake, you could even fish for your food. As a warning, always check that you are hunting in a legal field and obtain a relative permit or license. So, ask for information from the forest rangers in your local area before indulging in hunting activities.

Consider how you will be in control of what you are consuming, whether foraging or hunting. After all, you never know what procedure the store-bought groceries underwent before landing on your table. However, if you are the one who hunts, gathers, and grows your food, you will always be aware of the processes.

### *Natural Remedies for Short and Long Term Results*

Alternative medicine is related to off-the-grid life. Nature contributes with its medication, and most of us forget this valuable attribute. It is not to say you ought to replace medical assistance entirely. But why would you take artificial pills when you can take them from the soil and have the same results? Here's a summary of herbs you can take advantage of.

Aloe Vera produces a gel that serves for skin irritation. Simply cut the leaf into two and apply the slime to the infected body area. Flowers are not only pretty, but they also do marvels to the body. The dried leaves of Feverfew reduce migraines, headaches, and fever. It also works for indigestion.

What about using seasoning elements to cure yourself? Turmeric is an anti-inflammatory. Moreover, when transformed into an oil, it combats different fungus types, like athlete's foot.

Garlic functions as an antibacterial and antifungal; it stimulates blood circulation.

Peppermint also helps you with simple pains. Discomfort in your throat and congestion can be relieved by drinking a cup of tea with this plant. Even muscle aches and indigestion can be alleviated.

Take a chance with chamomile to deal with stress, anxiety, and depression and simultaneously treat infections. A tea made with the chamomile flower and taken before bed will give you a peaceful night's sleep.

With so many options to choose from, starting an off-grid lifestyle cannot be considered an option. Rather, it should be normalized as an everyday activity. After all, there are no excuses not to plant your food or reduce the use of electric devices. Moving to a landscape and forgetting about running water and heat is no easy task. It is understandable if people feel it is too much of a change. However, adding one or two of these projects to your daily activities is possible. They will enrich your life. But remember, this is just the beginning. There is more to this lifestyle and more activities you can add. Let's dig deeper into them.

# Chapter 2

## Rain Barrels

Water is a crucial aspect of survival. Whether for your crops, washing, or staying hydrated, you'll need a way to collect water to sustain yourself or your harvests. Self-sustained living couldn't be possible without it, and if you're living off-grid, finding ways to harvest water through rainwater collection will be your top priority.

You might be currently living off the grid, planning to live off the grid, or want to know more about self-sustained living because you're in a location without access to public water supply facilities. Finding ways to harvest rainwater is a viable option for maintaining an off-the-grid lifestyle or as a way to save energy consumption. The process can provide clean and fresh water to drink, wash clothes, water your garden and even give your home water pressure directly into your facilities.

An independent and safe water source is crucially necessary for maintaining survival and promoting autonomy away from 'the system.'

Enter the rain barrel. A rain barrel is an inexpensive and easy-to-use structure to collect and store rainwater from a downspout and drains the water into the barrel as it rains. It can also be left anywhere outside to sit and collect water through the opening. They hold up to 55-gallons of water and are often produced from food-grade plastic - perfect for flexibility and portability, recycled plastics - for the environmentally friendly, or wood - for those preferring to stay clear of artificially produced materials. A rain barrel collects water and stores it for daily use, emergencies during drought, or for homeowners looking for more environmentally friendly ways to wash cars or water their garden.

Harvesting rainwater was initially used to collect water during water shortages. Lately, the technique has been used by people wanting to live a sustainable lifestyle without reliance on public utilities. Using rain barrels to collect rainwater and use it as your primary water source is an effective strategy for off-the-grid living.

Before we go into the different methods to collect rainwater, it's important to consider your location. If you need a large water supply, your barrels must be in an area with lots of heavy rainfall. You don't necessarily have to live in this particular climate; you could always leave your barrels somewhere safe, let them gather water, and transport the full barrels back to your living location.

Another thing to consider is if your location doesn't experience rainfall for months during the summer, how will you collect rainwater? It might be necessary to consider diversifying your rainwater collection locations to create more than one water supply.

If you live in an area that experiences frequent downpours, you're already on your way to harvesting rainwater using any of the following strategies.

## Benefits of Rainwater Harvesting

- Independent, self-sustained water supply

- Rainwater is the eco-friendliest way to consume water

- Free water supply

- Various collection systems for specific needs

- Some collection systems can be dismantled and re-used elsewhere

- Inexpensive equipment

- Benefits gardens and crops due to lack of chlorine

- Easy to assemble and maintain

- Save on water expenses

Proper design and installation methods are integral to successful rainwater collection, and the techniques you use will depend on your specific needs. You might need a system for daily use, cooking or washing purposes, or larger enterprises - a monthly supply may be necessary for long-term sustainability.

## Methods of Harvesting Rainwater

### *Water Butt*

A water butt is a small or large outside storage container that collects rainwater from natural rainfall or drains guttering. Available in various sizes from 100 liters to 13,000 liters and are perfect for domestic use like gardening or everyday water necessities if used with a purifier. They come with a pre-installed tap, or you can attach your extraction method by drilling or cutting a hole into the base for easy access to the collected water.

If you decide a water butt is for you, there are a few things to contemplate when installing the container, for example, where you will leave it. You could collect rainwater by leaving the container somewhere out of the way and waiting for it to gather rainwater without any external water gathering technique. You could also use a draining system that collects the rainwater from an extended position and lets the water drain down into the tank. Both are relatively easy options you can use depending on your needs. Consider using more than one water butt and collecting rainwater using both of these techniques if you need to collect and store a lot of water.

When deciding which water butt to use, consider how much water you need. The prospect of a large tank may offset your off-the-grid lifestyle because the larger the tank, the more expensive it will be to install and maintain, although most of these tanks are made from 100% recycled plastic. Unless you decide to make your own, you're good to go by following these simple installation steps.

1.  Place the water butt directly beneath the downpipe connected to your guttering if using the drainage system.

2.  If the downpipe is too low, use a hacksaw or another sawing tool and cut the downpipe level to the top of the water butt.

3.  Measure and drill or cut a hole at the back spot where the downpipe connects to the top of the water butt and drill a hole for a water butt connector.

4.  Design your own or use a ready-made water butt connecter and diverter (if store-bought, fittings are provided), and attach the piece to the water butt. Ensure the connecting part is fixed and secure to prevent leaking.

5.  Drill or cut a hole into the bottom front of the water butt and install a faucet if you prefer to regulate the water flow.

To complete your new harvesting system, purchase a gutter filter to prevent debris, leaves, or dirt from draining into the tank. If you're committed to off-the-grid living, consider an old pair of tights or other thin material to act as a filter.

### *Underground Direct Feed (Submersed Pump)*

A submersible direct-pumped system is best suited for general household use or storing larger quantities of water, depending on your needs. This system pumps water from the container directly into bathroom facilities and can hold up to 22,000 liters. If you have the facilities and knowledge, you can build your own pumping system. For safety and efficiency, consider buying a ready-made harvesting system and follow these steps to install it.

1. Measure the width, depth, and length of the tank (for leeway, add 18"- 20"), and excavate the exact measurements from the ground, ensuring a maximum of 45" cover over the top of the tank.

2. Prepare the base of the hole by removing any debris and creating a flat, solid surface, ensuring the surrounding area is condensed to avoid falling mud or debris.

3. Place the tank into the hole, ensuring it is secure and fixed in place.

4. Install a pump inside the tank, as per instructions and feed a flexible pipe from the pump through the tank's opening and connect the pipe to your water mains.

### *Underground Direct Feed (Suction Pump)*

This system differs from the submersible system. The pump is located inside the property where the harvested water is needed. Use this method if you're still relying on your main water supply but don't want to overuse it, as this system will use your main water supply if the tank is low on water.

### *Underground Indirect Feed (Pumped/Gravity)*

This method uses the same techniques as described above, but instead of pumping rainwater directly into your preferred appliance, the pump inside the tank pumps the water into a header tank located inside the property. The header tank is connected via two attachments. One comes from the harvested rainwater tank, and the other feeds into the appliance requiring the water, like the bathroom facilities or washing machine. Using booster pumps to adjust the amount and pressure can control water usage completely. Place the header pump as high as possible (the higher, the better) and let gravity do its thing as it flows water down from the header pump into your appliance pumped from the harvested water tank outside.

### *Indirect Gravity*

This system is similar to the above. The harvested water is pumped into the header tank and placed at an extended height. Instead of using a booster pump for pressurized water production, the water is left to fall into your facilities. This method requires only the main pump generated from the harvesting tank.

As you can see, there is a huge range of rainwater harvesting systems available for collecting rainwater. Each method depends solely on the amount of water you'll need, how much exterior space you have to store a container or tank, and how many resources are available. Suppose a water butt is too small and a pumping system too large or not feasible. In that case, a water barrel is most likely the best method to collect rainwater because of its easy-to-install design and storage capacity.

## Types of Rain Barrels

### *Roughneck Rain Barrel*

Install and use your personalized water system for absolute self-sustainable living and convenient water access. You can buy a ready-made container or make your own rain barrel from a garbage can, and the great thing about these is they come with a removable lid. Then, all you need to do is follow these simple DIY steps.

1. Place your chosen barren beneath a downpipe. If the barrel is too tall, use a hacksaw to cut the drainpipe to sit directly above the barrel's opening.

2. Drill or cut a hole into the bottom front of the barrel and install a faucet if you prefer to regulate the water flow.

3. Place a net, screen, or other thin material over the barrel's opening to prevent debris or insects from falling into the barrel.

4. If your barrel isn't store-bought, it most likely won't have a lid, or there isn't an opening for the rainwater to flow into the barrel. In this case, cut or saw a hole into the top of the lid for downpipe access, place the lid over your preferred screening option, and you're good to go.

### *Solar-Powered Rain Barrels*

For the environmentally friendly, solar-powered rain barrels offer a greener method of collecting and using rainwater through a natural energy source like the sun. Use a solar-powered water pump for pressurized water flow for your garden, irrigation, or other water needs. It is easy to set up and install. A water pump is connected to the energy supply controller and left inside the water barrel to create pressurized water flow connected to a gardening hose or output feature of your choice. This water harvesting option offers an eco-friendly water supply and is perfect for an off-the-grid lifestyle. Keep an eye out for instructions on creating your own off-the-grid water supply in a later article.

### *Portable Rain Barrel*

If you're looking at options for harvesting rainwater for daily usage and portability, you need to consider practicality when choosing the right rainwater barrel. A portable rain barrel can hold up to 230 liters, is foldable for convenience, and doesn't need much preparation. Merely unfold and place beneath your preferred rainwater draining method (property downspout or DIY rainwater collector). The barrel also has a pre-installed faucet for accessible water flow and a mesh top to catch those pesky mosquitoes or falling debris. It's perfect for those with limited space or intermittent rainwater harvesting.

***Eco-Friendly Rain Barrel (Wood and 100% Recycled)***

A staple of traditional materials, wooden rain barrels offer functionality and durability and are an eco-friendly alternative to modern plastic material used in other rain barrel manufacturing. Although expensive to buy and more upkeep is needed, this option provides a classic style to any outside environment - you could even use an old whiskey barrel. They come in various sizes and collect water using the same method as the portable rain barrel.

Increase your use of natural resources and try an eco-friendly rain barrel made from 100% recycled plastic. These barrels come in various sizes, with some having a flat back so you can place them against a wall when space is lacking.

## Things to Consider

Although rain barrels cater to various water harvesting needs, a few things should be considered before installing one, especially if you're making your barrel from scratch.

**Materials:** When using a plastic rain barrel, check what plastic the barrel is made from. 100% recycled plastic is recommended, but if you're opposed to buying and plan on up-cycling a currently owned plastic barrel, check the plastic is BPA-free if you're using this harvesting method for drinking water.

**Wildlife and Childproof:** A large water barrel may be a perfect water source but dangerous for children or pets. Ensure the barrel is topple-proof and always covered.

**Size:** The larger the rain barrel, the heavier it will be when filled with rainwater, so size isn't always the most critical factor when considering your choice of a rain barrel. Consider the prospect of squandering rainwater if your off-the-grid lifestyle involves traveling. A large water barrel filled with water might have to be poured out as you travel to a different location. Although various sizes are available, it's beneficial to think about using more than one small or middle-sized barrel.

**Screen or Mesh Filter:** Prevent dirt, debris, insects, wildlife, and leaves from falling into your rain barrel by using a thin material and adhering it in place with nails or staples.

**Level Ground:** Don't let that precious rainwater build-up go to waste, so ensure the ground you place the barrel on is level and compact to prevent spillage.

You've chosen the harvesting system to use and remembered to consider all sizing options and safety prevention methods. After the effort involved in installing and collecting rainwater, you're thirsty and need to access the collected rainwater.

As discussed above, the steps involved in installing rainwater storage with a pump have many benefits, but the process is complex. Generally, you'll need the services of a qualified plumber to take care of this method's more complicated aspects. Nonetheless, it is essential for you to know all the steps involved, including the distribution process, to make an informed decision best suited to your needs.

Distributing water from your storage option involves different methods depending on your chosen rainwater collection method. Most of the options we have discussed come with a DIY or pre-installed faucet at the bottom of the tank, but for larger harvesting systems, a hand or electric pump is required to pump the water from the tank into your point-of-use.

**Gravity:** Let gravity do its job and collect your rainwater as it falls from the faucet, or the hose connected to the bottom of the barrel.

**Siphon:** Siphon water from an open-topped barrel with a bowl or large container, depending on your usage needs.

**Hand Pump:** A hand pump conserves energy consumption and is a valuable tool to distribute your water when you need it. However, it won't generate enough pressure to deliver water into your house.

**Electric Pump:** If you're using a large underground pumping system, an electric pump can generate enough power to distribute water into your house - as described above.

## Water Purification Methods

If you're living off-grid, purified drinking water will be the most important thing you need to prevent illness or toxins. While some rainwater harvesting methods are perfect for landscape watering or household items needing water to operate, other smaller methods are ideal for harvesting drinking water.

Firstly, you'll need a water purification system. Many options are available but choosing the right one for your needs is essential to benefit your off-the-grid lifestyle. Plenty of stores offer ready-made water purification systems, but these often require frequent replacement of particular parts, and this prospect may offset your self-sustaining philosophy. Luckily, you can implement a few different ways to make your water purification method using inexpensive and accessible items like sand, gravel, and charcoal.

**Sand Filter Purification:** Use for taste and debris. On top of your mesh filter, create layers of sand and gravel. Another mesh filter should separate each layer. Aim to create 3-4 layers.

**Charcoal and Sand:** Use for chemical purification. On top of your mesh filter, create sand, gravel, and charcoal layers. Another mesh filter should separate each layer. Aim to create 3-4 layers.

As you can see, there are more than enough rainwater harvesting methods to use for off-the-grid water supply. Let's go over the two main system options again.

1. Underground storage for large quantities of water to facilitate a household container relies on a suction or submersible style pump, which pulls water from the harvesting tank into a header tank. Then a booster pump flushes the water into your home as and when you need it.

   The downside to this method is you're relying on power to generate the pump. If your off-the-grid philosophy is completely independent living, this option is probably not the best for you.

   Unless you prefer a harvesting method mixture of equal parts pump and gravity, the system is similar to the above, except the header tank is extended as high as possible. The water flows down due to gravity.

2. For less complex methods of harvesting water, relying on free-falling water into rain barrels is by far the easiest and most accessible method for your water source.

The best thing about this method is mobility and adaptability. Get a foldable rain barrel and carry it around with you on your travels. Use a wooden or recycled plastic barrel and place them anywhere within range of a downpour of water. Place a few in different locations and get as much water as possible.

To live a self-sustained, off-the-grid lifestyle, all you need is a bit of knowledge, a few easy-to-find supplies for harvesting water, and you've got yourself the most powerful survival system in the world.

# Chapter 3

## Raising Chickens

Chickens have been domesticated for over 8,000 years and are a consistent food resource for people worldwide. Before KFC and pre-packaged poultry, our ancestors raised and used this livestock as a food resource when no other option was available, so there's no reason you can't either. Raising chickens as a food source will be an integral factor in the success of your off-grid lifestyle.

Raising chickens will be your most essential aspect of getting food if you're looking for ways to facilitate self-sustained living. Aside from meat and eggs, chickens are an important aspect of off-the-grid living, and they provide many additional benefits to your land that you are probably not aware of.

Easy to maintain, for the most part (we'll go into protecting them later), they're also self-sufficient in survival. You don't have to live on a farm to raise them; you can keep them in your backyard or the middle of the city as long as they have free-range living conditions.

These quirky, feathery friends are popular with farmers and livestock hobbyists. With the correct information, you too can reap the benefits of fresh eggs and poultry and even start your own business by selling their eggs.

Caring for a flock of chickens is different from raising a dog or cat, so before you become a chicken owner, let's look at some of the added benefits and necessities needed to raise your chickens and create a plan for your new venue to be successful.

## Benefits of Raising Chickens

### *Free Range Eggs and Meat*

Forget store sell-by-date or wondering about the sourcing and production process; with your chickens, you'll know they've been produced with healthy and ethical techniques. One of the best-known benefits of chickens is their eggs. Rich in vitamins and

Omega- fatty acids, you'll never go back once you taste your own sourced eggs.

Of course, eggs aren't the only food source to gain from keeping chickens. Meat from chickens can feed a whole family and produce an extra income if sold on the market. The resultant food tastes better with added health benefits by controlling what your livestock eat and how they live.

***Pest Control and Natural Fertilizer***

These feathery friends aren't only perfect for your food source. They also act as excellent garden maintenance. As they roam around their habitat, they peck at the ground swallowing up those pesky insects harmful to your garden and crops, like parasites, snails, mosquitoes, and other critters that cause damage to plant life.

Another fantastic benefit to keeping chickens is their ability to fertilize the soil. The best aspect is they'll do it continuously; you won't have to train or force them to do it. As they peck around, they control the weeds growing on your land, and simultaneously the soil is loosened, allowing for better growth of your crops and plants.

Imagine you have a particular part of the land you need to fertilize; simply corner off that area, put your chickens inside, and let them live happy with plenty of food and water. The nitrogen levels in chicken manure contain enough natural fertilizer to improve the growth and maintain healthy plants in a garden in less than a month.

The more chickens you have, the more fertilized your ground will be, saving you time, money, and resources.

### Low Maintenance

As long as your chickens are fed, watered, and kept in sustainable conditions, they will care for themselves. The effort put into housing and procuring them will be worth your time once everything is set up. You'll still have to be on the lookout for predators and disease and maintain cleanliness, but maintaining their home is a relatively low-maintenance method for off-the-grid living, especially considering their other benefits.

### Entertainment and Personal Pride

We're all familiar with the sound and vision of chicken flocks, even if we've never had them ourselves. For example, cinema uses livestock to liven up a film scene as background scenery in films set in the countryside. Their lively energy and curious nature can create hours of fun for you and your family. Take a time out, step into the backyard and enjoy watching them as they play and explore. It's also been proven that spending time with animals can reduce stress, making this livestock a natural mood-booster.

A sense of pride comes with raising, maintaining, and using chickens to survive away from societal norms. Once you get used to the fundamentals, you'll discover new ways to benefit from raising chickens, leading to happy and healthy living.

*Improve Off-the-Grid Lifestyle*

If you want to improve your self-sustained lifestyle, raising chickens is a great way to provide food, cut down on food production gas emissions, and reduce your carbon footprint by eradicating food transportation.

Raising chickens and relying on them for food benefits your health in ways you wouldn't have access to if buying from the local store. The protein, nutrient-rich meat from chicken and eggs are great for a healthy diet, supporting bone health and weight loss.

## Things to Consider

All progressives should understand the many positives of raising chickens, and, as beneficial as it sounds, there are still a few more factors to consider before jumping straight in.

*Noise Factor*

It's imperative to consider the noise factor when raising your chickens in an urban area. Particularly when the rooster crows in the early hours of the morning, your neighbors might not be as welcoming to your feathered friends.

*Legal Issues and Requirements*

Keeping chickens requires certain legal regulations and conditions you must consider, depending on your location. To get the best comprehensive legal information, contact your local authority and find their framework for keeping livestock and poultry.

- Conditions differ from country to country, and you might need to register your livestock and the functionality of your keep.

- Proper outdoor construction must abide by specific legal requirements

- Some countries require livestock to be vaccinated

- Sometimes, your local authority will have regulations on the number of chickens you are allowed to keep

Although there are different laws and restrictions regarding raising and keeping chicken, don't let the legalities deter you. As long as you keep yourself up to date on the legal requirements, there's no reason you won't live a successful off-the-grid lifestyle.

## Tasks and Requirements of Keeping Chickens

Maintaining a flock of chickens will involve daily and long-term considerations. Specific upkeep tasks will need to be done daily, while others will be important with long-term care.

### Basic Daily Care Requirements

- Set aside a minimum of 20 minutes every morning to check on their well-being (sometimes they get bored and bicker with each other)

- Ensure their feeding stations are stocked, and water features are full

- Set aside a minimum of 20 minutes at night to ensure they have all they need during the hours when you won't be available

- Adjust light requirements necessary for during the winter. Artificial lights will be required during the shorter days because chickens require around 15 hours of daylight to produce photoperiodic hormones to induce healthy egg-laying.

***Weekly and Monthly Tasks***

Set aside time for weekly cleaning chores. A few hours will be necessary to maintain a few chickens, but if you plan on having more, you'll need to spend more time dedicated to your cleaning routine.

- Changing the bedding inside your coop will need to occur monthly

- Soiled nest boxes create unhealthy living environments, so change these whenever they become soiled with manure or broken eggs

- Sanitize water containers at least every month

Besides the tasks involved in keeping chicken, you must also consider how much space you have available. Regardless of the overall space to fit the number of chickens, you also need individual measurements.

Each fully grown adult chicken will need at least two square feet of shelter space and another three square feet for an outside area to run around in; active chickens are necessary for health and food benefits. Their coop will also need to be at least three square feet high, but for this, you'll need to consider how much space you'll need for accessible cleaning.

## Items Needed to Build a Chicken Coop

So, you've considered the benefits, legal requirements, and issues for raising your chickens, and now it's time to look at how to build your very own backyard chicken coop to house your new feathered friends. A straightforward four-foot by six-foot coop could take up to a week to design, considering all the necessary components. You'll need a few essentials for building your coop and housing your livestock. It doesn't have to be expensive or complicated. So, let the DIY adventure begin.

### *Chicken Coop Structure*

- Coop structure: ensure you have enough space to house the chickens

- Size: at least three square feet for each chicken (inside the coop)

- Location: level the ground and make sure it's dry and away from high-intensity heat

- Convenience: you'll need to make it accessible for cleaning and upkeep

- Materials: wood, plastic, and PVC are the most common materials used for a chicken coop foundation, but make sure to use durable and non-toxic elements

*Chicken Coop Interior*

- Perch with at least ten inches all round

- Water drinking device

- Feeding device

- Nest box at least one square foot per chicken

- Temperature control

- Outside chicken run at least 25 square feet

- Toys for entertainment

- Electricity during winter

- Ventilation is crucial to avoiding disease

## Building a Chicken Coop

The following design plan is a simple four feet by six feet chicken coop. Feel free to optimize depending on your needs. There's no need to start from scratch; you could transform an old shed.

## 1.  Pre-Building the Coop

Always build a chicken coop on dry ground to ensure a solid base for the foundation. Remove all debris from the ground and consider overhanging trees or bushes to cut back if they grow in the way or house potential predators and insects. Remove or replace them if necessary.

## 2.  Choosing the Coop Design

As long as you've considered all aspects of a chicken coop, this factor shouldn't take too long to decide. It is the most critical aspect of ensuring your chickens have enough space. The great thing about keeping chickens is there are plenty of design options to choose from. Finding the right fit for your new adventure will be easy between small and large, raised or ground level.

Depending on your skills and knowledge about DIY, the larger the coop, the more time it will take to build, so keep that in mind when looking at the different options. Remember, your design doesn't have to be pretty. As long as your chickens have everything they need, it doesn't matter what the coop looks like, only that it does the job and provides sufficient shelter.

## 3.  Building the Coop Frame

For a four-foot by six-foot coop, you'll need 18 pieces of plywood for the frame and eight pieces for the roof. Measure and cut to your preferred height beforehand, taking into account the size of the roof, which will be angular. Ensure to use sturdy materials for this job; you'll need the coop to be as secure, durable, and weatherproof as possible. If you're using second-hand material, check for any rot or damage to prevent things from going wrong in the future. Also, think about the exterior; as mentioned above, your coop doesn't need to be pretty but at least consider protection varnish or wood treatment.

## 4. Attaching the Coop Walls

Use plywood panels as walls for the coop and measure and cut to your preferred size and lay them flush along the edges of the frame, ensuring no gaps, then fasten them to the frame. You'll need at least three-quarters of the coop covered with mesh for ventilation, so only a quarter of the frame will need plywood for the walls.

## 5. Laying Down the Coop Floor

You might decide to put flooring down; you don't have to, but it can prevent muddy wellies and ensure a drier coop environment. Don't worry if the floor isn't even, as long as it is secure and well-fitted, without any gaps or too extreme a slant. For measures to prevent insects or burrowing pests, ensure the wood you choose is smooth, without any groves for bugs to nest in. It's also an excellent measure to place mesh on the ground before laying down the flooring, so predators can't burrow through the floor.

## 6. Adding the Coop Doors

Don't forget about adding a door for yourself when building their new home with the chickens on your mind. You'll need a door for them and one for you. It doesn't have to be a house-sized door, as long as you can comfortably get in and out.

The entrance size for your feathery friend will depend on the quantity of the livestock you choose to keep (more on that later), but for now, consider their size and add a few inches on either side for potential growth.

Whatever entrance style you build, it's essential to create a secure entrance to prevent predators from creeping inside and stability during harsh weather. Some coop owners build a door to keep their chickens inside during the night and open it during the day. Others will leave an open entrance and lay mesh over the door frame. Ventilation is a top priority, so consider building a door frame from plywood and lining it with mesh.

## 7.  Building Furniture for the Coop

Nesting boxes will be home for chickens to sleep and lay their eggs and can be made from any box, as long as it is sturdy and stuffed with bedding. Consensus tells us to share one nesting box between three chickens; they love sleeping at a height, so for the perches, use a 2x4 piece of plywood with enough space for perched, happy chickens.

These were the basic steps involved in building a chicken coop. Hopefully, they have given you a better understanding of what materials you will need and some essential things to consider before choosing the design you need. Many chicken coop design options to choose from, so having a good idea of what you need is essential for off-the-grid living.

Now it's time for the exciting part of considering raising chickens: the actual chickens. Here are a few breeds to choose from for your needs and how to care for them.

- **Warm, Humid Climate:** Look for Mediterranean breeds such as White-faced Black Spanish, Minorca, Ancona, Leghorn, Catalana, Sicilian Buttercup

- **Cold, Harsh Climate:** Look for breeds such as Dominique, Australorp, Wyandotte, Buckeye, Chantecler, Orpington

- **Egg-Laying Breeds:** Look for breeds such as Cochin, Sussex, Leghorn, Wyandotte, Maran, Plymouth Rock

- **Temperament:** For small breeds, look for Silkie, Favarolle, or Cochins. Buff Orpington, Australorp, or Brahmas for docile and friendly breeds.

- **Designer Breeds**: Marans, Cochin, Ameraucana, Faverolle, Frizzle, Polish

- **Dual-Purpose Breeds**: For egg-laying and meat, consider Buckeye, Jersey Giant, Barred Rock, Black Star, Speckled Sussex, Chantecler

So, you've built your chicken coop and chosen one or a few of your preferred breeds; now it's time to consider the best practices for raising chicks into fully functioning adult chickens for successful egg collection. We have already covered most of the necessities for raising and maintaining chickens, but a few more things must be considered to ensure young chicks are protected and cared for properly.

A brooding box is similar to a nesting box in its material, but it needs to be big enough, so chicks don't jump out and draft-free for protection against the elements. Fill the box with enough food and water to keep them healthy. Chicks need to be fed crumbled starter feed increasing weekly as they grow.

Bedding and warmth: ensure to lay lots of bedding in the brooding box; chicks don't grow adequate feather protection until they're about six or seven weeks old, so they will need lots of warmth to survive. An electric heater or lamp is recommended to control the temperature on colder nights - aim for a temperature of around 35 degrees.

Once your chicks have grown into healthy adults, they will be ready to lay eggs; usually around 18 weeks. Depending on the breed, you can expect a daily supply of eggs. You will need to collect the eggs every morning to prevent broken eggs from spreading bacteria and creating illness.

Collecting eggs: carefully collect eggs from their nesting box once they leave their laying spot - use food as a strategy if your chicken is stubborn. As mentioned, collect eggs every morning.

Preparing eggs: try not to wash eggs in water - eggshells have a natural 'bloom' layer to protect the egg from bacteria. Instead, wipe the eggs with a dry cloth. Store them in a dry, ambient temperature location or the fridge for up to a month.

Raising, protecting, and rearing chickens is a rewarding personal adventure. Creating your own food (and entertainment) source, you're living a life that few can achieve or even dream of achieving themselves. To ensure you're on the right path, let's go over the essentials.

1. Raising chickens provides access to two types of food that promote better health

2. They are a perfect source of entertainment, are natural fertilizers, effective at pest control, and boost mood

3. There are possible legal requirements to consider depending on your location and local authority

4. Your new family will need daily care, so consider the long-term implications involved in raising chickens

5. The chicken coop needs to be sturdy, roomy, safe, and have good ventilation

6. Choose your chicken breed based on your location (some chickens fare better in warmer or colder climates), personal needs, and preferred temperament

7. Special care is needed for chick survival

This article has covered the basics of keeping livestock for off-the-grid-living, but it's essential to do extensive research before embarking on this journey. It's also necessary to think about what breed of chickens you want, depending on your food needs. To conclude, ensure you'll have the time to care for your new feathery friends each morning. Their happiness is vital for yours too.

# Chapter 4

## Solar Power

Humans have become dependable on electric and electronic appliances and devices in their daily lives, and now it is extremely difficult to stop using them. These technological advancements helped people do their daily tasks and errands faster and more efficiently. Living off-the-grid needs a source of energy to power up appliances and devices. However, our dependability on fossil fuels has affected the environment, causing diverse effects on the whole world. The green area of Earth has shrunk significantly in the last century, and the air and water pollution levels have soared and killed countless animals and plants.

Scientists started looking for fossil fuel replacements, which led to harnessing the sun's power, and that's how solar power became a valid alternative for fossil fuels. Solar energy is green renewable energy getting more popular over time for its various benefits for the environment and health. It is practical for an off-the-grid lifestyle as procuring fossil fuel will cost more money and waste time. Setting up a solar power system might be a complicated process but an excellent investment. Today it is easier and more affordable to build your own solar system than a decade ago, as the demand for solar alternatives has become higher recently.

Although solar power has existed since the 80s of the last century, many people still don't know or have little information about it. If you enjoy living off the grid or planning to do so, you need to know about this renewable energy source to make your life easier and your wallet happier. First, let's learn what solar power is and how we can use it.

## What Is Solar Power?

Solar power is generated by harnessing the sun's light and heat through solar panels. Theoretically, the amount of energy generated from the sunlight in one and a half hours is enough to cover the whole world's energy needs for a year. However, the technological advancements in solar power aren't enough to reach that goal for the time being. Solar technologies use solar panels or photovoltaic cells to convert sunlight or heat into electric energy. The harvested energy is stored in solar batteries or thermal storage and used directly for powering electrical appliances and devices.

Solar power may be the only feasible and reliable way to have electricity in their cabin or RV for people living off the grid. The cost of connecting to the grid will be insanely expensive and, in most cases, not an option as the nearest grid is usually miles away from where you want to stay. It is essential to know that installing a solar system is expensive, but sellers offer payment plans making it more affordable. However, affordability is not the only reason to purchase or build a solar power system.

## How Important Is Solar Power for Living Off-the-Grid?

As mentioned before, being the only feasible option makes solar power important for anyone living off-the-grid. However, there are many benefits to using solar energy in your daily life.

### *No Power Outages*

Losing electricity is common, especially in rural areas, as storms, strong winds, and freezing rain can damage power lines and equipment. Weather conditions also overload the electric transformers and cables, which leads to power outages. Living without electricity causes inconveniences that will bother you in the short term, and in the long run, it is stressful anticipating the worst all the time. Solar systems or solar-powered devices and appliances are reliable as they get their energy even in cloudy conditions. Moreover, they store energy so it can be used at any time. You will suffer power outages if you forget to store energy or if the sun doesn't come up for a couple of days.

### Electricity Bill Reduction

Fossil fuels remain the main source of energy around the world. However, as they deplete, these resources, such as petroleum, oil, natural gas, and coal, become more expensive as their prices keep going higher and higher. Consumer electricity bills equally keep getting higher as well. Solar power doesn't have the same future as fossil fuels because it is an infinite energy source. While the initial cost of installing a solar power system is relatively expensive, you will save time in the long run as you will never have to pay for any electricity bills. Additionally, the system is an investment as it doesn't lose its value and can stay functional for 20 years without any replacements.

### Easy to Install

The cost of installing a solar system can be high as many people use the services of solar power professionals for the installation. It may seem like a complicated process, but the truth is anyone with the right set of tools can do it themselves. Installing the system yourself will lower the cost of installation significantly. Research must be done to know what equipment and parts are required to install a solar system. Depending on your budget, you can install a basic solar system or a state-of-the-art one.

### Environment-Friendly

We all know how much damage fossil fuels have caused the environment. Animals, plants, humans, and the Earth is dying from our carbon footprint. Therefore, many countries and environmentalists encourage people to switch to environmental-friendly renewable energy sources. If you are conscious about your carbon footprint and want to help fix the environment, using renewable energy sources, such as solar, wind, and hydro, will positively affect the world.

## What Is a Solar Photovoltaic System?

The term "photovoltaic" comes from the cells that construct the solar panels, called photovoltaic cells (PV). The sun emits sunlight or heat radiation; the PV cells absorb this radiation and turn it into energy. The PV system is responsible for collecting energy from the sun and turning it into electricity that you can use at home and consists of several parts besides the solar panels. There are several steps to convert sun energy to electricity:

1. The sunlight hits the solar panels creating an electric field. The photovoltaic cells transform this energy into a direct current (DC). The electricity generated from each panel flows to the edge of the panel and into a conductive wire.

2. A DC switch is installed to turn off the flow of electricity for safety reasons if needed.

3. DC power is unsuitable for appliances and devices like washing machines or laptops. Therefore, the inverter in a solar system is extremely important as it converts the

DC electricity coming from the solar panels into alternating current (AC).

4. The AC power generated from the inverter is routed to a battery or fuse box. Solar energy batteries usually store DC electricity, meaning that when this energy is used, it will go through the inverter again.

5. The electricity flowing to the fuse box will go through an electricity meter. Although the electricity meter is optional, it is useful to know your electricity consumption to be aware of what you're using and calculate how to consume less energy. For solar systems connected to the grid, the electricity meter also shows the amount of power the system transfers to the grid.

6. The fuse box is responsible for directing the current to power outlets around the house to power appliances or devices.

## How to Make PV Solar Panels

You can build PV solar panels at home and even the whole system. However, it requires excellent craftsmanship skills to avoid breakdowns and faulty parts. The second concern is finding the right materials to build the panels, as high-quality materials will produce better results than low-quality ones. Additionally, low-quality materials can cause damage to the panels or start a fire, which is highly dangerous and destructive. However, if you have the skills and the materials, all you need is to follow these steps to build PV solar panels.

### *Step 1: Building a Frame to Support Solar Cells*

Solar cells are installed on a frame to support and protect them from thermal and mechanical tensions. The frame protects the fragile cells and is used as the last step's mounting attachment. It must be made from non-conductive materials, such as wood, plywood, plastic, or glass, so it doesn't interfere with the cells and their wiring. When cutting the frame, measure the dimensions of the solar cells and cut the board to that size. However, leave an extra couple of inches at both ends of the board. You will connect the wires that come out of each row together in that space. Wood is a popular material to use as a frame because it is easier to drill through than other materials. Cell wires will pass through the holes drilled in the frame.

### *Step 2: Purchasing Solar Cells*

Before purchasing solar cells from the first website or store, you must know the different solar cells and decide which ones are suitable for your needs. Various solar cells are available. But the most popular and suitable for commercial use are monocrystalline, polycrystalline, and thin-film solar cells. The monocrystalline and polycrystalline cells are made from silicon. Monocrystalline cells are made from single crystalline silicon and have a circular shape with dark blue color. They have the highest efficiency rate among other solar cells reaching above 20% in newer models. Their high-efficiency rate means they have a high power output, take less space, and last longer than other solar cells. They perform well in cloudy conditions and withstand hot temperatures more than polycrystalline cells. However, all these advantages come with a high price tag.

Polycrystalline solar cells' angles are not cut like the monocrystalline cells. They are square-shaped and distinctive by their blue speckled look. They are more affordable than monocrystalline cells as they are made by melting raw silicon, which is a faster and more affordable manufacturing process. However, the process affects their efficiency rate, which reaches 15%. These cells take more space to generate the same power output as monocrystalline cells and are more affected by hot temperatures. Although they are less efficient than monocrystalline cells, the difference between both cells isn't notable. Polycrystalline cells are considered the best cost-to-efficiency option in the market.

Thin-film solar cells are the most affordable option among the photovoltaic panels. They are manufactured by placing several thin layers of photovoltaic materials such as silicon, copper, and cadmium on top of each other to create a panel. Hot temperatures have less effect on these solar cells, and they are flexible, which means they have various applications. However, these cells take a lot of space to generate power deeming them unsuitable for residential installations. They have less efficiency rate of 7% to 13% and a very short lifespan. Depending on your budget and the space available for solar panels, you can determine which option is more suitable.

The solar cells offered in the market are plenty, but the high-quality ones are made in the United States, Japan, or China. The number of solar cells you need should be calculated based on the energy you want to generate. Consider that solar cells are extremely fragile, so buy extra cells if one of them breaks while manufacturing the panels. Whether you buy the cells online or from a local store, they usually come with a protective wax cover. Remove the wax first by dipping the cells in hot but not boiling water. The cost of each cell shouldn't exceed $2 per watt.

### Step 3: Tabbing the Solar Cells

This whole step is shippable if you buy pre-tabbed solar cells. Skipping this step will save you time, but these cells are usually more expensive than non-tabbed cells. Tabbing solar cells means connecting each solar cell to the next one to create a solar module. This process can pose some health hazards, so precautionary measures must be taken before starting it. Wear gloves with a good feel while handling the solar cells as they are so fragile. Soldering can cause solder and fumes to fly everywhere, so wearing a mask and safety glasses is crucial to protect yourself.

To tab solar cells, solder a wire to the contact points of the cell. Start with placing the cell in a clean space with its negative side facing upwards. Grab a flex pen and rub it on the two vertical lines (the contact strips) that run up and down the solar cell. Measure and cut tabbing wire pieces with their length equal to twice the cell's height. For example, if the solar cell is 3 inches high, the tabbing wire pieces should measure 6 inches. The tabbing wire pieces are placed on the contact strips. Heat a soldering iron and solder the pieces to the cell; the tabbing wire should be already coated with solder.

### *Step 4: Testing the Solar Cell*

Before going further with the manufacturing of the solar panel, some tests must be conducted on the cells to ensure none of them are defective. A defective solar cell will negatively impact the power output of the whole panel. The solar cells should be tested for their voltage and current by placing them in the sunlight. Get your multimeter and plug its black lead into the black port and its red lead into the voltage port for the voltage reading. Plug the red lead into the amps' port to get the current reading. Place the solar cell on a clean surface with its positive side facing up. Connect the multimeter's black lead to the cell's negative contact and the red lead to the positive contact. For a standard 1.75-watt solar cell, the voltage value should be around 0.5 volts, and the current value about 3.5 amps. If the values are less than these readings, the solar cell is probably defective and must be replaced.

### *Step 5: Gluing and Connecting the Solar Cells*

After tabbing each cell and making sure two tabbing wires are coming out of the cell, apply glue to the center of a cell and press it gently on the backing board. The tabbing pieces should move freely. Solar cells must be connected in series for the maximum voltage value. When connecting two cells, make sure there is a small space between them, a minimum of 0.25 inches. Like in batteries, the negative side of a cell should connect to the positive side of the next cell. The top side of a cell is the negative side, and the bottom is the positive side. Connect enough cells to generate a minimum voltage of 12 to 24 volts in one row. After connecting every cell to the row, test them to ensure they are working properly.

Once you have finished the first row, solder tabbing wires to the front side of the first cell that extend to the gap on the end of the board, these two tabbing wires will be soldered together with a piece of bus wire that has the same length as the distance between the thick lines of the solar cell. At the end of the first row, put a piece of bus wire that covers two rows. Connect the last cell of the first row and the first cell of the second row to this bus wire. Repeat this step for each row you add. You will connect the last solar cell to a short bus wire in the last row.

### Step 6: Preparing the Panel Box

Measure your solar panel and cut a piece of plywood to the same size but add 1 inch to every side to install the sides on this extra inch. You will need non-conductive planks to build the sides. Measure and cut 1 inch by 2 inches pieces to cover the long sides of the panel. You will need another two 1-inch by 2 inches sides to connect the long pieces together using screws. Screw the sides to the bottom of the box and the long sides to the short sides. It is advisable to paint the box sides with white or reflective colors to keep the solar cells cool during the day.

### Step 7: Wiring the Panel

Once you have finalized the panel box preparation, connect the last row's bus wire to a diode bigger than the amperage of your solar panel and secure them together with silicone. The diode has a light-colored side and a plain side, and the plain side is connected to your panel. This step can be skipped if you have a junction box with a built-in blocking diode. If not, connect the diode and the other end of the panel to the junction box. You will need to purchase a charge controller, a battery, and an inverter.

The charge controller prevents the current from going back to the PV panels, especially at night. However, in some solar systems, the charge controller is not needed. The batteries are essential for storing excess electricity generated by the panels. The inverter is a must as it converts DC to AC, and all appliances and devices must use AC electricity. You decide if you want all these components according to your budget.

If you opted to buy a charge controller, connect the wires from your panel's junction box to the charge controller in the right plugs. Afterward, connect the charge controller to a solar system battery. The battery is then connected to the inverter.

### *Step 8: Finishing the Solar Panel Box*

To protect your solar panel from the elements, you need to put it on a clear sheet of acrylic or Plexiglas. The protective piece must be cut to fit inside the box. Acrylic and Plexiglas sheets are preferred as they are durable and weatherproof. You need to get 1-inch by 1-inch blocks of wood that will be put in the box's corners. Use wood glue to secure the wooden blocks in the box. Put the protective sheet carefully on these blocks and carefully screw them into the block. Finally, use a silicone sealant to seal the edges of the box to ensure the panel is closed, and nothing can get inside.

### *Step 9: Mount the Solar Panel*

The panel is ready for deployment, and you choose where you want to install it, whether on the roof or on racks. Secure the panel tightly so the wind will not knock it over, and it will be ready to function.

## Solar-Powered Applications

Harvesting solar power from the sun is not only about generating electricity for homes. Some appliances, vehicles, devices, and small constructions can be powered using solar panels. Here are some innovative applications of solar power.

### *Solar-Powered Lawnmower*

If you have already built a solar panel, you will have the tools and materials needed to build a solar-powered lawnmower. Consider that if you have a gas lawnmower, you will have to change the motor to an electric one. You need to construct two 12-volt solar panels to mount on the lawnmower. Check the lawnmower battery's condition; you may need to change it to one compatible with solar panels. The wiring between the batteries, the solar panel, and the motor is very similar to building the solar panel. You have to mount the solar panels on the lawnmower, and it will be good to go.

### *Solar-Powered Herb Garden*

Powering your herb garden with solar power isn't any different from powering your house with it. Calculate the amount of electricity you need to meet the power requirements of your garden. Purchase or build solar panels to generate the desired electricity. If you already have an herb garden, place the panels facing the sun to get the most out of them. When you build your herb garden, choose the position carefully so it is oriented toward the sun. Your herbs will use the sunlight for growth, and the solar panels generate electricity.

The future of energy and humanity is in making the most of renewable energy. This energy is environmental-friendly and infinite, which makes it the ideal energy source to rely on. Governments and individuals are moving to solar energy to reduce their expenses and save the environment. Solar technology is still in its preliminary stages, but it has huge potential with a lot of research dedicated to exploring its applications. Living off-the-grid requires that people satisfy their needs, such as food, water, and energy. That's why solar power is perfect for living off the grid, as you can harvest the sun's power and use it to power your house.

Solar panels use the sun's radiation to convert it into electricity. It may sound complicated to build your solar panels, but with the right supplies and tools, you can build one easily in a short time. Although it is expensive to install a solar system, the prices are getting lower each day as the materials are getting cheaper and the demand is higher. Solar systems save money on electricity bills and increase property value in the long run. There is no doubt that solar power is the future for living off the grid, all of humanity, and sustainable living.

# Chapter 5

# Wind Power

The wind is simply the flow of air caused by the upward and downward movement of pressure in different regions. Between 1979 and 2010, it was estimated that the average amount of wind energy in the world was 1.50 MJ/m2, with the Southern Hemisphere an estimate of 1.70 MJ/m2 and the Northern Hemisphere an estimate of 1.31 MJ/m2.

Wind energy, known as wind power, is the term used to refer to the kinetic energy produced by the movement of air, more commonly known as wind. Wind energy is the energy extracted from the wind and then transformed into a form that can be used to generate electricity utilizing wind turbines. Compared to mechanical energy, which necessitates the combustion of fossil fuels, the impact of wind energy on the surrounding ecosystem is significantly less damaging.

Wind energy is a variable and sustainable renewable energy source that applies management strategies to control the amount of power generated.

Some techniques for managing wind power include using excess capacity, wind hybrid power systems, hydroelectric power and other power dispatch sources, geographically distributed turbines, grid storage, and the export and import of power to surrounding environments. As the energy generated by wind power continues to rise, a greater need for an upgrade to the grid that supplies and distributes the electrical energy generated by wind power is required.

A weather forecast is used to anticipate changes in wind power production, and then an electric power network is prepared in advance of those changes. Both these outcomes are possible thanks to wind power.

## How Is Wind Kinetic Energy Produced?

The process of heat absorption creates wind kinetic energy at high temperatures and heat release at low temperatures. This heat absorption and release process are made possible by the atmosphere's ability to function as a thermal engine. As a result, wind kinetic energy is produced at a rate of 2.46 W/m2, sustaining atmospheric circulation against friction.

A wind resource assessment can estimate the global wind power potential of any region, area, or country. The Technical University of Denmark, in partnership with the World Bank, created a Global Wind Atlas that assesses wind power potential around the world.

Certain tools also provide a time-varying simulation of wind speed and power density from various wind turbine models per hour. This is more efficient than using 'static' wind resource atlases, which can only estimate wind speed and power output over several years. In addition, specialist commercial providers and larger wind developers with in-house modeling capabilities can provide more detailed assessments of wind resource potential specific to sites.

The total amount of power extracted from wind for economic purposes is much greater than the total power generated by all human-made power sources combined. Wind energy is variable energy because wind strength varies. The amount of energy produced by a wind turbine at a given location is determined by more than just the average value for that location.

A probability distribution function is usually the best method for analyzing wind speed data to evaluate prospective wind power sites. There is a different wind speed distribution for each location. The Weibull model best represents the actual distribution of hourly per ten-minute wind speeds at several locations. Since the Weibull factor is usually close to 2, a simpler model is the Rayleigh distribution; however, it is less accurate.

## The Difference between Wind Energy and Solar Energy

### *Wind Energy*

### *Pros*

- Wind energy is generated whether at night or during the day

- It is a clean source of fuel that causes no harm to the environment

- Wind turbines convert more than half of wind energy into usable power. The largest wind turbines can generate enough electric power to power 600 homes

- Wind turbines will work regardless of the direction they face

- Wind turbines can be built onshore and offshore

- It is a domestic energy source

- It does not cost anything to produce and is cost-effective

*Cons*

- Wind may not move fast enough to turn the turbines. But equally, it could also move too fast and damage the turbines.

- Wind turbines require regular maintenance. Only professionals can do the maintenance.

- Lightning can damage wind turbines.

- Wind turbines can hurt or kill flying creatures like bats and birds

- Wind turbines are not suitable for residential areas because of the noise it produces

- Some people might consider wind turbines as a visual disturbance because of their height

- Since most wind farms (collection of wind turbines) are built in rural areas, electricity can't be generated if transmission lines aren't built

### *Solar Energy*

Solar energy makes electricity generation possible using the heat or light of the sun.

### *Pros*

- Since the sun reaches almost every area, solar installation is possible at any location.

- Allows you to use the energy for light (PV) or heat (CSP)

- It saves land space since panels can be mounted on rooftops and are suitable for urban areas

- Panels mounted on rooftops allow for generated power to be distributed, creating an electricity grid that is diverse and resilient

- Technologies operate silently and are therefore good for populated areas

- Don't require much maintenance

- Easy to generate and transport

- Panels work under hot and cold temperatures

- Reduces the cost of electricity as the power generated is almost free once the panels are installed.

- Panels are renewable

- Panels are reliable

- Quick installation of panels

- Excess energy generated can be sold to utility companies.

*Cons*

- It cannot be produced in cloudy areas or at night

- The direction the panels are installed impacts their efficiency

- Panels are expensive

- It is expensive to store excess energy using batteries

- CSP systems, which allow solar energy even when there is little or no sun, are more expensive than PV systems.

- Solar panels only convert 14 percent of available energy to power. A larger installation area is needed to increase the percentage.

## Wind Turbines

Wind turbines are mechanical devices resembling windmills but with blades that rotate in the opposite direction. When the blades rotate, they capture and channel air currents, allowing them to transmit mechanical energy along a driving shaft. The shaft then acts as a generator, converting mechanical energy into electrical energy for your home, decreasing the money you spend on your monthly electric bills. Wind turbine assembly is not a difficult task.

Before moving on to build an energy-producing wind turbine, there are a few things you must address.

**Determine the Average Wind Speed of Your Building Site:** To generate electricity the most cost-effectively, you must ascertain that the wind speed in your location is between 7 and 10 miles per hour or 11 and 16 km per hour. A wind turbine will function best when the wind speed is between 12 and 20 m/h or between 19 and 32 km/h.

**Find Out about Building Regulations for Turbines**: Building wind turbines is subject to many regulations across the country. A few regulations detail the minimum distance between the turbines and the minimum distance between the turbines and residential property. Additionally, the height of the turbines is usually specified, and it is essential to be aware of these requirements before constructing a turbine so that you do not run afoul of any laws.

**Assessment of Turbine Spacing**: There is no significant room needed for a wind turbine. If the turbine produces approximately 3 kW of power, position it at least 0.2 hectares away from any property located in the surrounding area. If it generates approximately 10 kilowatts of power, it must be situated at least 0.4 hectares away from residential areas. The wind turbines should also be placed at a higher elevation than any nearby buildings or trees that could impede wind flow.

**Pick between DIY Wind Turbine Blades or Pre-made Blades**: You can construct or purchase your turbine's blades. Make the blades out of a PVC pipe if you want to make your wind turbine. No matter which option you decide to go with, it is strongly recommended that your wind turbine have no more than three blades.

**Choose a Generator:** The turbines must be connected to generators for electricity produced by wind turbines. In addition, to convert direct current (DC) from generators into the alternating current (AC) required by most home electronics, the generators need to be connected to an inverter.

## Step-By-Step Instructions on How to Build an Energy-Producing Wind Turbine

Below is a step-by-step guide to building a wind turbine.

### *Step 1: Assembling the Spokes and Spindle of a Vertical Axis Wind Turbine*

**Assemble the Spindle:** When you buy a wind turbine kit, you will notice that the spindle has been welded onto the spindle plate. This will allow the spindle to rotate freely. If this is not the case, you can weld it yourself. When constructing a wind turbine, it is recommended to build the spindle first. Then, you can proceed to add the remaining components.

**Slide the Hub into the Spindle:** You must first install a bearing in the space between the spindle and the hub to reduce the friction. Place the hub on top of the bearing so that the studs face upward. Then slide the bearing over the end of your spindle to face the spindle plate. Check that the bearing fits into the thick area of the spindle.

**Attach the Lower Spoke Flange to the Hub:** Slide the studs of your hub into the holes on the flange, ensuring the flange is resting evenly on the hub. Once this is done, you can fasten the studs with nuts. Tighten the nuts using your hands first and then a socket wrench to firmly hold them.

**Connect Spokes:** Each turbine blade has two sets of spokes. Use bolts to connect those spokes to the lower flange tabs and separate the upper spokes from the lower spokes using spacers.

Put a bolt through a hole on the flange tab, fit your spoke into place on the bolt, and place a spacer on the bolt. Then, fit the second spoke on the bolt before placing the upper flange to sandwich the spokes and spacer. Screw in the bolt with the upper flange and fasten the screw. Do this for all the spokes.

Tighten all the bolts using a socket wrench when you are done sandwiching the upper and lower flanges. The spokes and the upper and lower flanges should be strong and spin easily alongside the hub.

**Attach Four Studs to the Upper Flange:** The ideal specs for the studs should be 6cm long with a thickness of 635 cm and must be threaded. Distribute the studs evenly on the spindle shaft and screw each stud into the upper flange by hand. The studs should stick out of the upper flange by an even length. If you cut the threaded rod yourself, ensure that the thread is not damaged because it can prevent you from fastening the parts appropriately.

### Step 2: Mounting the Magnets

**Place the Lower Magnet Rotor on Studs:** Magnet rotors are made with epoxy rotor plates or 2 in x 1 in x 1/2 in neodymium magnets. You can also purchase it as a part of a turbine kit. If you use neodymium magnets for your magnet rotor, get 24 (12 on top of your magnet and 12 below) since they are annealed.

**Make a Magnet Rotor:** This step is not necessary if the turbine kit you purchased comes with a magnet rotor, in which case you will only need to place the rotor on the studs. However, if you make a magnet rotor yourself, make sure that the magnets are distributed evenly around the rotor edge. Use a marker to note the polarity of the magnets before you place them on the rotor.

**Place Spacers on Your Studs:** To create spaces, use a metal tubing of exactly 0.375 cm to cut into a long segment of about 3.175 cm. Place the spacers on top of the studs that stick out of your magnet rotor. Ensure that all the spacers are evenly cut to prevent the upper magnet disk from slanting.

**Place Stators on Your Lower Magnet Rotor**: Stators are wires wound into coils and are an integral component of any generator. You can get them as a part of a turbine kit or make them yourself locally. It is important that the stator is centered on the central spindle shaft and that it encircles the part of the studs that stick out from the outside of the central spindle shaft. The stator should be made up of three clusters, each with three coils made of 24-gauge copper wires. The copper wires on each coil must be wound 320 times in total.

**Make a Stator Winder:** You can complete this task with plywood and nails. First, use the nails to connect the two pieces of plywood (one at the top and the other at the bottom). The nails must not be driven too deeply into the wood. They must be spaced out in the shape of a rectangle, with the distances between them corresponding to the dimensions printed on the magnets. As a result, winding the copper wire will be easy.

Place a piece of colored tape at the beginning and end of each coil to make it easier to track them. In addition, tape some of the coils together before securing them with two-part epoxy. This will prevent the coil from unraveling further.

**Place Your Upper Magnet Rotor:** You must proceed with extreme care during this stage as it is the most hazardous. First, arrange the boards on your stator so that they are stacked so that they are touching the two ends of the central spindle (the upper boards should be thin with the lower boards thicker). The upper boards ought to have dimensions of 2 by 4 inches.

Keep your hand in between the stacked boards to support the upper magnet rotor as you lower your upper rotor gradually toward the lower rotor while aligning your upper rotor to the studs. Once the upper rotor is in place, remove your hand. The magnetic field must exert enough force to pull the upper rotor down onto the boards. To lower the upper magnet rotor onto the studs, slide the boards out one at a time in opposite directions.

Continue the same procedure for the lower boards to ensure that the upper magnet rotor is installed correctly. Install the rotor by screwing hex nuts onto the studs and securing them. The upper rotors will continue to be supported by the spacers, and only a fraction of the studs will be visible above the surface. If you wiggle the boards in both directions, you should be able to dislodge them from the upper magnet rotor.

### Step 3: Turbine Assembly Finishing

**Detach the Spindle from the Assembly:** The next stage begins with connecting the spindle with a tower. This goal will be impossible if the spindle is still connected to the turbine assembly (hub, spokes, magnet rotors, stator, and other parts). Position the assembly so that the hub's top faces the direction you will be working after removing it from the spindle by raising it until it slips off.

**Weld the Spindle Flange to the Tower**: This modification has already been made on a turbine kit. On the other hand, if you choose to construct the wind turbine on your own, you will need to construct the tower out of a metal plate connected to a robust metal pipe. The pipe needs to have a sufficiently thick wall to withstand gusts of wind, and it also needs to be installed in an area where the ground is sturdy enough to support it. For example, you could support the tower by constructing a concrete slab around it.

**Install Bracket for Stator and Spindle:** Install a bracket with a collar-like fitting on your spindle. Fasten the bracket to the tower first, then bolt the two structures together. Following that, cut a 0.375-centimeter-long threaded rod into 4 and 1/2 pieces. Using a thread locking compound, nuts, and washers, secure the threaded rod to the outer area of your bracket so that the upturned end faces outward. Next, install the nuts on the threaded rod studs about three-quarters of the way down the road. This allows you to adjust the stator's position while the rod holds it in place.

**Place Greased Bearing on the Spindle:** Apply all-purpose grease with your hands to cover the bearing and slide it into place to completely flat with the bottom of the spindle.

**Attach the Main Assembly of the Turbine:** Place the main assembly on top of the spindle with the hub facing upwards. Make sure there is a tapered bearing underneath the main assembly. It is important that the threaded rod studs attached to the bracket align with the mounting holes on the stator.

After the assembly has been properly positioned, a second oiled bearing should be attached to the hub cap. Then, use your fingers to secure a castle nut on top of the bearing, ensuring that the hole is properly aligned with the hole in the spindle shaft. To secure the castle nut, first, insert a cotter pin into the hole and then use pliers to bend the pin's legs to secure the castle nut.

**Fasten the Stator and Place a Grease Cap:** Use a hex nut for each rod to fasten the stator firmly on the assembly. With two wrenches, keep adjusting the hex nuts so that the stator becomes sandwiched directly between the magnet rotors. Then, add a grease cap to your hub to complete the turbine.

## Examples of Other Projects Done with Wind Power

### *El Algodon Alto, 200-MW Wind Farm*

This is a 200-MW wind farm that RWE Renewables developed. It is powered by 91 Vestas turbines capable of generating enough electricity to power up 60,000 homes. It is located in San Patricio County, Texas. The project is already in operation.

### *200-MW Golden Hills Wind Farm*

This is a 200-MW wind project that Avangrid Renewables developed. It is located in Sherman County, Oregon. The amount of electric energy Puget Sound Energy (PSE) generates is enough to power 60,000 homes every year. The wind farm went online on the 29th of April 2022. The project supports the reduction of PSE carbon dioxide emission and provides energy for periods when the electricity demand is high, like during winter.

### 300-MW Seven Cowboy Wind Project

This is a wind power project that Enel Green Power North America is developing. The location is in Kiowa County and Washita County, Oklahoma. With 107 turbines, it is expected to generate an energy of 1.3 TWh yearly, which should power 120,000 homes. It is said to go online by the end of 2022.

### Deerfield II Wind Project

This is a 112-MW wind project that Liberty, a subsidiary of Algonquin Power and Utilities, is developing, assisting the parent company of Facebook, Meta, in reaching its renewable energy goals. Commercial operations are set to begin in 2023. It is located adjacent to the Deerfield I wind facility in Huron County, Michigan.

### Sunrise Wind, 924-MW Wind Project

This wind project will use direct high-voltage current (HVDC) technology to support offshore wind. The project is a syndicate between Siemens Energy and Aker Solutions, and Siemens Energy will be providing the HDVC transmission. The project will generate enough energy to power 600,000 homes in New York. Its location will be over 30 miles east of Montauk Point, Long Island, and is estimated to go into operation in 2025.

### 1-GW Offshore Wind Farm

This is an offshore wind farm developed by Total Energies off the coast of North Carolina. It is a project expected to go online by the year 2030 and should be able to generate over 1 GW, which is enough energy to provide over 300,000 homes with power.

Wind power can contribute to the expansion of the economy significantly. Even though it is not a typical method of producing electricity, if there is enough public awareness rand government funding, it has the potential to become an extremely important part of the economy. This method of producing energy is already adopted in several different regions of the world, and it is expected that it will become widespread and a global energy source in the near future.

# Chapter 6

# Bee Farming

Bee farming is the care and maintenance of bees and their hives, otherwise known as Apiculture. The beekeeper is called an Apiarist, and the Apiary refers to the entire colony system. Beekeeping has received significant attention in recent years, and not only is honey high in demand but there is also an equally high demand for beeswax and royal jelly.

## The Importance of Keeping Bees

Whatever your motives are for deciding to keep bees, you must realize that it is both exciting and extremely important.

Bees are excellent pollinators. It is assumed that many crops are reliant on bees in some way or the other. Several crops rely heavily on bees, while others only rely on them partially. Strawberry, cashew, broccoli, pear, sunflower, raspberry, apple, and other fruits are a few crops that benefit from bee pollination. However, if bees disappeared, food would become boring and repetitive because there would be an absence of variety.

Bees contribute to the well-being of animal and plant species, thereby maintaining ecological balance. This variation is critical if our environment is to be well protected.

## The Economic Importance of Keeping Bees

Crops are an important source of income for farmers and crucial for overall economic growth. The number of crops that rely on pollinators rises every year as the human population grows. Bees play a crucial part in agricultural production, and beekeeping is an essential component of our agricultural production. Aside from crop plants that rely heavily on bees, the bee's existence increases plant quality and availability.

Commercial hives are leased seasonally to pollinate a variety of plants. As a result, production rates would drop, food prices would increase, and food production would be seriously affected if these services were not provided.

## Types of Beekeeping

### *Natural Beekeeping*

Natural beekeeping attempts to replicate the bees' local habitat. A beekeeper caters to the needs of bees using methods and approaches equivalent or similar to those in the wild and in their native form. Intrusion into the colony is kept to a minimum, and the beehive survives on honey alone; no sugar or external feed is provided. Bees prefer natural comb to premade or replicated comb.

Most beekeepers who practice organic beekeeping do not employ any treatment methods within the hive. However, essential oils are used to treat various conditions, including mites.

### *Backyard Beekeeping*

Backyard beekeeping is the practice of keeping beehives in an urban setting. It attempts to gain honey and other bee products through colonies. Backyard beekeeping is on the rise in several areas of the world.

### *Indoor Beekeeping*

As per the name, it entails bringing bee colonies inside due to a shortage of space, tracking needs, or it is the off-season. The most recent developments have created improved in-house colonies that provide a safe haven for bees to flourish. Many commercial beekeepers relocate their hives to storage facilities with constant moisture levels, light, and temperature during the cold weather. This improves the colonies' health.

## Choosing a Beehive

A beehive is a formation in which honeybees live and rear their young. Several hives are available, and the selection is based on personal preference.

Whether you want to start a honey production venture or merely try your luck at beekeeping, once you decide to start your own beehive, the first thing to obtain is the hive. The important question is whether you will set up or purchase a hive. It may be a simple choice for several beekeeping enthusiasts. However, for those who are unsure, consider all the pros and cons first.

## Buying a Beehive

Consider purchasing a completely prepared beehive if you are ready to start beekeeping. Then, you won't have to put yourself through the strain of conducting research and constructing a hive. Instead, your attention would be focused on the bees.

## Building Your Beehive

Why not construct a beehive if you fancy woodworking and have a little knowledge and skill? You will develop a wider understanding of your hive's internal structure and increase your likelihood of beekeeping success. In addition, you get to save cash. However, based on the hive you construct, you will still need to purchase materials and possibly some components. You can also purchase a beehive set that includes all the beehive components, and it is relatively easy to install.

You must only purchase parts or components from a credible seller to guarantee the highest quality components to make a proper, resilient beehive.

If you decide to paint your hive, choose a color that will reflect sunlight and prevent the hive from becoming too hot. Also, avoid painting inside the hive.

Constructing a beehive needs proper exploration and time based on your abilities, so plan in advance.

**How to Build a Beehive**

- You will need a razor, four clamps, a hammer, four hive boxes, and a carpenter's square to get started.

- Lay down the four hive box pieces next to each other and the nails required for their assembly.

- Examine the hive box components. Snip any edges that are too sharp or have splinters with a hacksaw blade or razor.

- If your box doesn't provide pre-drilled openings for nails, it is best to make a hole where the nail goes before proceeding. While this is unnecessary, it will keep the nail properly positioned when you hammer the box together.

- Fit all the hive pieces together to form a box and make sure they fit firmly together before permanently attaching them.

- Working your way up, attach each clamp to every side of the box. This will keep it in place while nailing it. Even though the box might be well nailed without each of the four clamps, it is simply not advisable. The clamps make it much easier to nail the box together by keeping the pieces in position while you drive nails through them.

- You can begin by driving nails through the box. Choose a top edge and nail it.

- Proceed to nail the other two edges similarly.

- You can now begin nailing the sides of the box. Begin with one side of the box and navigate your way around it.

## Types of Bees

### 1. Worker Bees

Every worker bee is born infertile and female with the sole purpose of working for the rest of their lives. They are the hive's backbone. Even though they are females, they don't possess the queen's abilities.

### 2.  Drone Bees

Drone bees are male with a singular objective in the colony of mating with the queen bee to breed offspring. However, this is a difficult job because the queen eventually kills all drones by removing their sex organs and keeping the sperm in her body.

### 3.  Queen Bee

Every beehive needs a queen to ensure the colony is filled by laying eggs. Her sole purpose is to produce offspring. Others are required for hive preservation, honey production, and caring for their queen.

## The Best Hive Location

Choosing an appropriate location for your beehive is an important aspect of apiculture. The location of a beehive determines whether or not a colony thrives. Safety and accessibility must be considered when deciding on an apiary location because you don't want your honeybees jeopardized while also ensuring easy access. Also, think about water availability because bees require a constant water supply. Other factors to consider for the best location include local regulations, sunlight, and shade.

### 1.  The Langstroth Hive

The Langstroth hive is unarguably the most widely used in present apiculture. It is made up of an exterior and interior cover, frames, honey supers, a base, an offspring compartment, and a queen excluder. It is heavy and moving the colonies can be difficult.

### 2.  Top Bar Hive

This hive is made up of wooden bars stacked on top of a large box. Honeybees construct honeycombs from top bars. It is lightweight and easier to manage compared to the Langstroth hive. However, because a honey extractor cannot be used to harvest honey, you must remove the comb from the bar. Therefore, bees must build a new comb every year.

### 3.  The Warre Hive

It is known as a "parallel top bar hive." It comprises identically sized stacked boxes without panels or base sheets. Honeybees construct combs out of top bars positioned in every box. Warre hives are relatively smaller compared to top-bar and Langstroth hives. Fresh boxes are added beneath the current boxes when bees require more space.

## How to Keep Your Bee Colony Safe from Predators

Bees' ability to protect themselves is remarkable, and their defense mechanism keeps evolving to keep them safe from natural dangers. However, they will occasionally require your assistance in combating bee predators. The following suggestions are examples of methods you can use to keep your beehives safe from predators.

### 1.  Your Hive Should Be Enclosed

Fencing is a simple way to keep dangerous animals away from your hives. Integrate hot barb wire to keep paws off your valuable beehive.

### 2.  Your Beehive Must Be Kept off the Ground

Skunks will be discouraged from trying to get into your hive if you raise it several feet above the ground. They do not want to be stung in the stomach.

### 3.  Spike Strip

This may appear harsh, but it has served many beekeepers. Construct a deck with needles or tacks protruding upward to keep animals away from the hive.

### 4.  Robbing Screens

These screens keep wasps or bee wolves out of the colony while allowing resident bees to enter and exit. Insect pests that do not reside in the beehive are confused by the screen since they can smell the honey and will attempt to invade it. The screen teaches those leaving the hive how to exit while keeping trespassers at bay.

## 5. Reduction of the Entrance

These small entrances allow multiple honeybees to gain entry, but not bigger pests like wasps. Most beekeepers use entrance reducers, which are mainly made of wood and placed at the doorway to the hive to narrow the entrance. Metals and plastics can be used if wood is not available.

## 6. Natural Repellants

You can also investigate odors that some predators find unpleasant. Certain oils from several organisms can discourage predators from entering your hive. These repellants include peppermints, garlic water, lavender oil, camphor, and vinegar.

## How to Protect Your Bees in Hot Weather

### *The Source of Water*

Water is essential for keeping the hive cool. Honeybees capture it in their honey guts and transport it back to the colony for a cooling effect. Bees are ridiculously picky about their water sources. Ensure your bees have a favorite water source.

### *Shade*

Providing shade is one of the easiest ways to reduce the temperature in your beehives. When warmer weather is forecasted, simply place a cover above your hive.

### *Proper Ventilation Is Essential*

Proper ventilation will save your hive from excessive heat and melting in hot weather. The best method for ventilating a hive is to create an upward entrance through which the heat can escape. If the honeybees don't use this opening, cover it with a piece of screen so hot air can escape, but predators cannot enter.

## How to Protect Your Bees in the Winter

### *Insulation*

Insulation is the most effective way to keep your colony warm. Typically, beekeepers use insulation in the warmer months to keep hives cool, but it can also keep colonies warm in cold weather. The coating under the roof particularly will assist in maintaining a stable temperature inside the hive even when the temperature outside is low. Consider installing an insulating material box. Insulation allows bees to maintain their natural breathing patterns. Other methods involve covering the hive with a rigid foam material or black in color. Both options are excellent heat conductors.

### *Enough Food*

Check to see if they have enough food for the colder months. You can help your bee population thrive by placing apples in water for them to drink or feeding them with sugar water.

## Beekeeping Calendar

Honeybee activity varies according to the season, so knowing the overall pattern of honeybee colonies is essential for effective planning. The nectar circulation is controlled by weather and follows different seasons. When nectar is plentiful, the colony produces more eggs, and the population grows. The colony's population drops when food is scarce.

### *Spring*

Fresh pollen and honeydew sources improve spawn rearing in the spring, and it is an ideal time to establish a new colony. If rations were reduced during the colder months, you might need to feed the bees in spring to increase egg hatching. The population explodes further towards the end of spring, so make sure there is enough space to avoid swarming at this point. If the honeybees outgrow the available space, they will undoubtedly swarm. You can encourage the storage of multiple resources by including empty frames.

### *Summer*

Summer is the best time to extract honey. The colony has reached its peak community, and all efforts are now concentrated on finding food and collecting honey. Honeybees require more space for honeydew storage; more space encourages nectar gathering.

### *Fall*

The colony is getting ready for winter, and you must make sure there are sufficient food reserves to last the winter. In addition, it allows for improved ventilation and installs safeguards against insects and rodents.

*Winter*

The colony is entirely reliant on the available resources. The activity of laying eggs and rearing offspring is halted, and the bees huddle together to generate heat. By removing the drones, the intake of the saved honey is reduced, and the bees might require sugar feeding. The colony also requires a protective barrier to cover it. It's essential to check if the bees and the queen bee are still alive at the end of winter.

## Tools and Equipment for Beekeeping

Safety is a top priority in apiculture. Bees can sting other living creatures in the vicinity of a hive or Apiary, so adequate safety precautions are required for undisrupted and smooth beekeeping. Honeybee stings can cause health issues, and if people or pets are harmed, legal action can be taken against the beekeeper. Therefore, handling the hive, Apiary, and overall area is essential for beekeeping. However, few important tools are required to make your job much easier.

*Smoker*

A smoker is a tool used by beekeepers to spread smoke into the colony. The fumes relax the bees and shield the alert pheromones of the guard bees. This disorder enables the beekeeper to access the colony and perform any task. Unfortunately, it also triggers the bees to start feeding. After feeding, a honeybee loses its capacity to sting.

*Hive Tool*

Like a paint remover tool, it aids in opening the hive, lifting frames, loosening hive components, and scraping off propolis and surplus wax. When accessing a hive, a hive tool is a must-have.

*Bee Brush*

A bee brush with long, soft fibers will help you remove honeybees stuck in panels and honey supers when extracting honey.

*Safety Gear*

Bee stings can be avoided by wearing safety clothing. A complete beekeeping jacket, protective eyewear, a mask, and boots are required. Coats and jackets are white because lighter shades are soothing to bees. Gloves are typically made from leather, slim and flexible, making them convenient and less likely to injure the bees.

*Utilizing Sugar Water*

Several beekeepers use sugar water to prevent bee stings, which has improved beekeeping safety. The introduction of sugar water as a vapor causes bees to begin grooming one another. Because the bees are invested in the sugar water, the beekeeper goes about his business at the hive.

## Harvesting Honey

Prepare ahead of time and avoid rushing the honey harvest. Delicate, peaceful motions, rather than overly dramatic movements, will aid in keeping the bees calm. Also, make sure you're not wearing any fragrance, cologne, or deodorant, as these will attract intrigued bees, making it difficult to work.

- Sturdy colonies are given additional hive boxes labeled "honey supers" to produce honey. These boxes include pre-formed honeycomb pieces. It is ready to harvest honey after the honeybees have covered the honey super and the comb with beeswax.

- However, do not take all the honey from the colony because you don't want your bees to go hungry during the cold season! Instead, take whatever is leftover or in the additional honey super.

- A fume board is the most convenient way to extract honey from a bee colony. Position the fume board on the upper end of the filled honey super you want to harvest honey from. After some time, the bees will become desensitized by the odor and abandon the honey super, allowing you to keep the honey box with the honey inside.

- Beekeepers frequently use a smoker to calm the bee colony but using more than necessary during extraction can change the taste of the honey.

- You can start the extraction procedure after removing the honey super from the colony and transferring it to a bee-free spot.

## The Challenges of Beekeeping

### *Bee Diseases*

Ailments spread rapidly in honeybee colonies and can destroy the entire colony in days. American foulbrood is by far the most dangerous brood disease. Chemicals and heat do not affect the bacteria. It is a global disaster. Numerous laws require the infected colonies to be burned. Chalkbrood, European foulbrood illness, and deformed bee virus are among the other ailments.

### *Parasites*

Wax moths, tracheal and varroa mites, and tiny hive beetles are the most popular bee parasites. Wax moths lay their eggs on honeycombs. When the larvae hatch, they burrow down the combs, ruining the honey stores. Hive beetles are extremely damaging and can cause a bee population to flee if attacked.

### *Predators*

Honey badgers are the most popular honeybee predators. They feed on honey, larvae, and sometimes even older bees. Rodents, geckos, and birds like bee-eaters are among the many predators.

## Beekeeping Tips

### 1. More Colonies Are Advisable

It is preferable to have multiple beehives rather than one for efficiency reasons. You can move honey, pollen, or brood from one colony to another when necessary. You can also easily boost a weak colony. It is easy to re-queen hives without a queen, and when necessary, the beehives serve as a replacement for one another. The re-queening of a beehive is an important task performed once every twelve to twenty-four months. You can raise another queen by purchasing a queen cage. This cage encloses the existing queen entirely, keeping her safe while also allowing you to identify her offspring when hatched.

## 2. Conduct an Inspection Every Week

A successful and fit hive quickly runs out of room. If there isn't enough space, the bees build queen cells and move in less than 14 days. Therefore, inspecting their colonies at least once every week is important.

## 3. Start in the Spring

The best time to begin beekeeping is in the spring, so there is enough time to establish, raise a brood, and store sufficient honey before the colder months.

Developing a backyard beekeeping adventure requires advanced planning. However, following the guidelines outlined in this article will decrease the likelihood of unexpected incidents, which is discouraging to new beekeepers.

When your bees have made it through the first year, you will finally be able to relax and enjoy Apiary, and before you know it, you will be harvesting honey.

# Chapter 7

## Farming

You live in the city. You love your fast-paced life and the convenience of getting anything you need with a few clicks of a button. But lately, you've been feeling the call of the country. You decide to set up an off-grid house in the calm and beautiful countryside. But, as soon as you start knowing more about the off-grid project, you are brought back to reality about how everything has to be self-reliant and environmentally friendly to achieve that status. One of the biggest concerns is food. How can we produce food sustainably, so we don't harm nature and at the same time lower our carbon footprint? The answer lies in understanding the true concept of off-the-grid farming. What goes into it, and how does it benefit us and the environment? Let's find out.

## What Is Off-the-Grid Farming?

Off-the-grid farming is agricultural farming where farmers produce food without relying on the public power grid. It means they are self-sufficient in energy and often use renewable resources like solar and wind power. However, off-the-grid doesn't mean you cannot use modern technology and the internet for growing your farm produce.

Off-the-grid farming is more environmentally friendly than any other traditional farming method. Our reliance on fossil fuels for energy is one of the biggest contributors to greenhouse gas emissions. By producing their own energy, off-the-grid farmers are doing their part to protect the environment by reducing their carbon footprint.

There are many benefits to off-the-grid farming, but it is essential to put the right infrastructure in place to run the farm properly. Many questions are relevant before we plan to build an off-the-grid farm. From energy generation that would feed all the farming systems, apart from your daily energy expenditure in other lifestyles and work, to building an energy storage infrastructure enabling operations at night or when any haphazard occurs to the main power source. Here is some important basic infrastructure that your farm would need.

### *Power Source*

One of the most important apparatuses for your off-the-grid farm is multiple sources of green energy. Renewable energy like solar and wind power is the go-to energy to generate electricity for your home and farm. Solar panels convert sunlight into electrical energy, while your wind turbine harnesses the wind's kinetic energy. But the most important thing one needs to figure out is the total energy expenditure of the farm. Considering and calculating the wattage of every appliance, from the water circulating motor to the fridge in the cold storage unit, will give you a clear indication of how much power you'll need to sustain and run your farm without any outage successfully. Once you have calculated the total wattage and running time, you can plan to buy power units accordingly for enough power to run the farm.

### *Energy Storage Infrastructure*

An energy storage unit is a must-have when planning an off-the-grid farm. A robust, integrated energy storage system provides consistent, seamless, and trouble-free power. These mechanisms are great for storing energy during the day to use it at night. This way, you don't have to worry about your farm being without power when the sun goes down. Plus, energy backup units are very helpful during power outages. If there's a storm or another emergency, you'll still have the power to keep your farm running smoothly.

### *Waste Management Mechanism*

Off-the-grid farms are not only about using green energy for survival. It's also about reusing and recycling waste to lower the net carbon footprint. And what better way to minimize waste from the farm to achieve that milestone. You can save millions of liters per month by reusing and treating water from livestock, fish tanks, dairy plants, and irrigation lines for the crops. Composting toilets and farm waste is another good idea. They don't require any water or electricity to operate and create nutrient-rich compost to fertilize your plants.

### *Cold Storage Unit*

Investing in an efficient cold storage unit is imperative to the success of an off-the-grid farm. It allows you to extend the growing season by preserving food that would otherwise spoil. Reports from FAO (Food and Agriculture Organization) suggest that using a cold storage unit helps minimize post-harvest loss by 85%. In addition, a cold storage unit helps you preserve surplus crops for times when there is a shortfall.

### *Efficient Water Distribution System*

Using a maintenance-free, highly efficient water pump to source water from various water sources like underground wells, rivers, or lakes to circulate to farming stacks and livestock units is essential for a farm. It provides a necessary source of hydration, but it also helps regulate temperature and remove waste products. With the intelligent installation of pipes and pumps, farmers can ensure that water is quickly and evenly distributed throughout their property. In addition, by circulating the water regularly, farmers will prevent stagnation and bacteria growth. Drip irrigation is a great way for distribution to water your plants without wasting water or taking up too much space.

### *Intelligent Use of Space*

Living Off-grid requires creativity and resourcefulness to make the most of what you have. You have to be very intentional about the way you use your space. It means systematic and intelligent use of every inch of your home and property space.

You can do a few things to make the most of your space and get the most out of your off-grid farm. First, consider what crops you want to grow and where they will grow best. You'll need to plan your planting around the sun, shade, and wind patterns on your property. Second, you need to employ the right farming techniques to produce a good yield without much space. Using vertical farming and building trellises, pergolas, and other structures will give you more room to grow without taking up valuable ground space.

## Farming Methods for Off-Grid Farms

Various farming methods go by the book to successfully become environmentally safe and sustainable. This farming practice is what an off-the-grid project needs to fulfill its aim. Some of the methods are

### *Kitchen Gardening*

Kitchen gardening merely grows fresh fruits, vegetables, and herbs in your property's backyard. This farming process is also known as a vegetable garden or nutrition garden. Kitchen gardening or farming produces fresh vegetables, herbs, and fruits utilizing the waste produced from the kitchen and free of any toxic pesticides.

It is also a wise way to manage space in your house property. Not only do you get fresh produce straight out of your backyard, but you are also efficiently using your waste and space, reducing the carbon footprint, and making the environment of your house even better. You need a sunny spot, good soil, water, and sunlight in your yard, and you can easily set up a kitchen garden. You can grow almost everything in a kitchen garden but choosing plants that do well in your climate is important. Tomatoes, peppers, eggplants, squash, beans, and herbs are all good choices.

You'll need some pots, containers, or baskets for growing your produce. Buying high-quality soil and good organic seeds to produce your vegetables and fruits is recommended when employing this farming technique. Also, use organic matter to help the soil hold moisture and nutrients and add a slow-release organic fertilizer to the soil before planting. Connect one of the irrigation water lines with the kitchen sink and smartly use your water distribution channel. Hence, none of the used water gets wasted. These efficient and intelligent techniques make it one of the ideal farming practices on off-grid farms.

### *Vertical Farming*

A vertical farming method is agriculture, where crops are cultivated in vertically stacked layers in a controlled environment. Crops are grown in rows on shelves or racks. The shelves are often made of plastic or metal and have drip irrigation built-in to provide water to the plants. The racks are usually stacked several stories high, and the plants are grown using artificial light. So, a stacked approach generates high farm produce yields in a very small space.

There are many reasons why off-the-grid farmers choose to grow crops using this method. It can be done in a smaller space than traditional farming methods, making it ideal for urban areas, rooftops, and off-grid projects where space usage must be very efficient. Additionally, because the environment is controlled, there is less need for fertilizers or pesticides and other chemicals harmful to the environment.

The control environment ensures there's much less chance of the product becoming stale or rotten than in traditional farming, where even a slight weather disruption can damage the crop. So, vertical farming is financially more attractive than traditional farming due to its high yield and minimal crop damage. Lastly, vertical farming allows farmers to grow crops year-round, regardless of outside weather. Many vertical farming versions are used around the world. Some of the most important are:

# *Hydroponics*

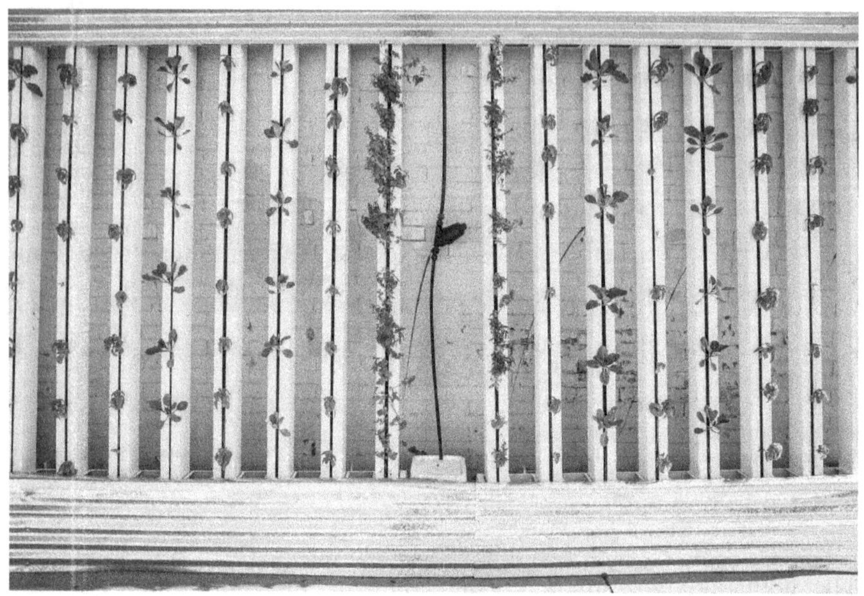

Hydroponics farming is agriculture where plants grow without soil but use mineral nutrient solutions in water. This farming method can grow various crops, including fruits, vegetables, and herbs. Hydroponics are operated in many ways, but the core principles of the farming technique remain the same.

Although these agricultural methods do not require soil, they still require something to support the plants' roots. This entails materials that retain moisture, like coconut fiber, perlite, and rock wool. There's also a constant need for a water supply with proper oxygen. Various nutrients like phosphorous, magnesium, and calcium naturally present in soil or fertilizers are supplied in water circulated among the plants. Due to this, hydroponics eliminates the use of soil.

The main benefits of hydroponics farming in off-grid farms are that it requires less water than traditional farming methods and is done in a controlled environment (a greenhouse). This means that crops are grown year-round, even in harsh climates. Additionally, because hydroponics doesn't need to use soil and is very space-efficient, it can be set up anywhere - including indoors and maximizes crop yield even on a small plot of land.

*Aquaponics*

Aquaponics is a farming system combining raising aquatic animals with hydroponics. It is a sustainable and efficient method to breed fresh fish and simultaneously grow vegetables and fruits using far less water than traditional methods.

In the aquaponics farming method, a large tank with aquatic life is allowed to breed in-house. These aquatic lives can vary from fish and prawns to mollusks. Food for the aquatic life is supplied in the tank, where the fish consumes the food and releases its feces. These feces and leftover food make the water ammonia-rich and are then passed through a biofilter before supplying the plants. The water becomes nitrogen nutrient-rich and is a nutritious growth solution for plants. The plants further act as a natural filter, cleaning the water before it is returned to the fish. This symbiotic relationship between the fish and plants provides a healthy environment and eliminates the need for chemicals or other artificial inputs. The controlled environment produces a shield that enables higher crop yields without any damage.

Aquaponics is more environmentally friendly than other food production methods and extremely rewarding. The combined output of farm produce and fisheries makes this farming a hit for off-grid farmers financially and sustainably. And to top it all, these systems can be set up indoors or outdoors, in any climate, and even incorporated into vertical spaces. They use far less water than other farming methods and produce food year-round. This versatile and resilient system provides you with fresh fish and vegetables with minimal effort on the farmer's part.

### *Aeroponics*

Aeroponics is a new method of growing plants in an air or mist environment without soil. It is derived from the Greek words for "air" and "work." Aeroponic systems are as simple as a mister nozzle attached to a timer that periodically sprays roots suspended in mid-air. Computer-controlled chamber constantly monitors and adjusts nutrient delivery to the plants.

Aeroponics is considered a hydroponics form because it uses water as the growing medium. However, aeroponics differs from other hydroponics. It does not rely on soil or other solid materials to support plant roots. Instead, roots are suspended in the air in a controlled environment, and nutrient-rich water is sprayed onto the plant's roots. This farming method is usually done as tower farming, where towers are erected with these plant saplings and a high-pressure atomizer or sprayer beneath them. Tower farming uses even less space than stack farming and yields similarly to hydroponics. However, aeroponics has the advantage of fewer pests and disease attacks due to the lack of contact between two plants. These advantages make it ideal for an off-grid farm.

## Crops That Can Be Grown in Limited Space

When growing food in a small space, it's important to carefully select the right mix of vegetables, fruit, and grains. Not all crops are equal in their space requirements, and some yield more food per square foot than others. For example, even though they require more room, vining crops like tomatoes and cucumbers produce more fruit than other plants. Likewise, leafy greens like spinach and lettuce occupy less space than heavier crops like corn and beans. By carefully choosing the right mix of crops, you can make the most efficient use of your limited growing area. These vegetables and fruits are the most widely grown in a small space

### 1. Tomatoes

Tomatoes are the perfect vegetable to grow in a small space on an off-grid farm. They grow using supports like trellises or tomato cages. Tomatoes don't require a lot of water or space, and they're relatively easy to care for. They're a versatile ingredient used in many dishes like salads, sandwiches, sauces, soups, and a good source of vitamins A and C.

## 2. Lettuce

You may not think of lettuce as an exciting vegetable. Still, it's a pretty awesome choice for small-space gardening. Not only does it grow quickly, but it can also be grown vertically, making it ideal for small farms and off-grid living. Lettuce is relatively low maintenance, so you spend little effort nurturing them. Perhaps, best of all, lettuce is packed with nutrients essential for good health.

## 3. Melons

Melons are vines. So, they easily grow in small areas, like pots, raised beds, or stacks. Melons are extremely drought tolerant, making them perfect for growing in dry climates or during times of drought. It also means they require very little water to grow. Moreover, they provide fresh, healthy food that can be stored and eaten throughout the year. Furthermore, they're a great source of income if you decide to sell them at farmers' markets or roadside stands.

## 4. Spinach

This leafy green is used in various dishes, and it's easy to grow using multiple vertical farming methods. It grows faster than other vegetables, so you get more bang for your buck in yield. Spinach is also a very nutrient-rich vegetable. It's packed with vitamins A and C and iron and calcium, ideal food for those improving their health.

## 5. Berries

Berries are a high-value crop and one of the most profitable assets for a farmer.

They're an ideal fruit to grow in small spaces for several reasons. Firstly, they are a very compact fruit, needing little ground space to produce a good crop. Secondly, the controlled environment makes them easy to care for. Thirdly, they offer a wide range of benefits, are excellent vitamins and minerals sources, and are low in calories. Berries have a range of health benefits, including improving circulation and boosting the immune system. As for their uses, berries are enjoyed fresh or in various recipes, from jams and jellies to pies and smoothies.

## 6. Beans and Peas

One of the best reasons beans and peas are perfect for farming in small spaces is they are excellent companions for other plants and improve your garden's health. They easily grow in trellis and pergolas setup with other weed vegetables. Lastly, bot beans and peas are a good source of vegetable protein and complement many sweet and savory dishes.

## 7. Basil, Cilantro, Chives

Herbs like cilantro, basil, and chives grow in small spaces for many reasons. You can easily tuck them into a corner of your kitchen or even on a windowsill. They don't require much watering or fertilizing and don't need much space to spread out. Most importantly, they are widely popular in cooking, decorations, and even natural pest control.

## 8.  Avocados

Avocados are nutritious and delicious fruit grown in a small space. Just three trees can produce up to 150 avocados a year, making them an ideal crop for backyard gardens or patio farms. In addition to their culinary uses, avocados offer many health benefits; They are an excellent source of fiber and vitamins C, E, and K, lower cholesterol, and promote healthy skin.

## 9.  Potatoes

Potatoes are a great option if you're tight on space but still want to grow your own food. They're relatively easy to grow in containers or raised beds in a small area. There are some great benefits to growing potatoes on an off-grid farm; they're ideal for small gardens or urban farms and naturally resistant to pests and diseases. So, you can feel good about growing them without using harmful chemicals.

## 10. Cucumbers

Cucumbers have a range of advantages, making them a must grow in your kitchen, backyard, or on off-grid farms. Eat them fresh, pickled, or even made into juice; you get many uses from a small yield. They can even tolerate some less-than-ideal growing conditions, perfect for homesteaders or off-grid farmers who might not have the time or resources to devote to a more demanding crop.

They're a great source of food for people and animals and as a natural fertilizer, improving the soil quality on your farm.

## Pest Control Methods for Off-the-Grid Farms

Fending off pests is a daunting task. But when farming off-grid, using traditional chemical pesticides to defeat pests would, in turn, defeat your purpose of becoming an environmentally friendly farm. There are many reasons to choose organic methods for pest control, especially when following a sustainable lifestyle. First, it's better for the environment. Second, it's better for your health. Third, it's more effective. And fourth, it's more economical in the long run. Below are a few of the many effective organic pest control options available.

### *Bio-Pesticides*

When farming off-grid, always look for ways to be more sustainable and reduce your impact on the environment. One way is using bio-pesticides. Bio-pesticides are made from natural materials and are more environmentally friendly than traditional pesticides. They are also more effective against specific pests to target problems more efficiently. In addition, bio-pesticides break down quickly in the environment and pose no risk to human health. So, if you're looking for a more sustainable way to farm, bio pesticides are worth considering.

### *Oil Spays*

You're working hard to build a self-reliant off-grid farm. Then pests show up and feast on your crops. What's can a farmer do?

Pesticides are one option, but most are full of harmful chemicals, and you don't want those in your food. The good news is that there is an organic option - pesticide oil sprays. These are made from natural ingredients like clove oil or garlic, and they're just as effective at defeating pests as the chemical-laden alternatives. They're better for the environment and won't harm you or your family if you eat produce treated with them.

### Using Pests to Control Pests

Using pests to fight pests in your off-grid farming operation or kitchen garden is a novel biological pest control method with real benefits. For example, certain wasps target specific caterpillars wreaking havoc on your plants. Similarly, ladybugs are natural predators of aphids and other small insects damaging your crops. So, using these beneficial insects is a much more environmentally friendly approach than spraying chemicals. In addition, using pests to fight pests reduces the overall population of harmful insects in your garden, making it a healthier place for your plants to thrive.

### Sticky Traps

You might not think of farming when you think of sticky traps, but these little guys are a big help with pest control. If you're off-grid or have a kitchen garden, sticky traps are a great way to keep pests from wreaking havoc on your crops. These traps attract pests with a sweet or pungent smell, then trap them on the sticky surface. This method is great because it's non-toxic and relatively low-maintenance - just set the traps and forget about them. Plus, sticky traps are effective against various pests, including flies, moths, and beetles.

### *Crop Rotation*

Crop rotation is a powerful tool in the fight against pests. This is accomplished by planting various crops in different areas from season to season. It confuses and starves pests that might otherwise decimate your plants. Crop rotation improves soil health by increasing nutrient levels and preventing erosion when done properly. As a result, crop rotation is an essential part of any off-grid or kitchen garden pest control strategy.

### *Intercropping*

It's imperative to be smart about pest control when growing a kitchen garden or farming off-grid. Intercropping is a great alternative because it uses natural mechanisms to repel pests. Planting certain crops next to each other confuses pests and makes finding their preferred food source difficult. Additionally, intercropping improves soil fertility and increases crop yields.

Well, there you have it! Everything you need to know about off-grid farming. Now that you know the basics start planning your off-grid farm. Of course, there's plenty more to learn, but this should give you a good foundation.

# Chapter 8

## Greenhouse

When living off the grid, cultivating food in a small area can be daunting. It's even a huge task when you don't make money from the produce. Greenhouses are the best bet for producing multiple crops under one roof. This farming technology results in high production yields. But what is a Greenhouse, and how does it work? Let's find out.

## What Is a Greenhouse?

A greenhouse is a farming facility made with a transparent roof and walls where plants are grown in controlled climatic conditions. It has a structure similar to a house, predominately made of glass or similar material that allows sunlight to enter. This quality allows greenhouses to maintain high temperatures even in cold weather and allow the farmers to grow tropical plants or other delicate plants that cannot tolerate frost.

The main goal of these structures is to create a microclimate favorable for the plants cultivated. These agricultural structures are most commonly used in areas with severe weather and where cultivating plants outdoors is not feasible. Greenhouses were originally only used in cold, severe climates, but advances in modern farming technology have resulted in operating them in hotter climatic regions.

In contemporary times, glasshouses come equipped with state-of-the-art temperature, light, humidity, and pressure stabilizers. These components micromanage the climatic requirement of the plant, raising the temperature and humidity automatically during winters and cooling it down during summers accordingly. The goal behind this mechanism and greenhouse is to enhance the farmer's capacity to produce crops all year without considering seasons.

Various greenhouses serve the same fundamental objective of providing plants with a warm, regulated environment. Greenhouses exist in various sizes and are determined by the agricultural enterprise's size. A low-cost greenhouse would have only a UV film affixed to the glass and a timber superstructure with no climate control, relying exclusively on the natural convection of sunlight flowing through the glass to keep the temperature stable. These glasshouses are typically located in backyards and used as a gardening hobby or to grow food for personal consumption.

A high-end glasshouse would be constructed around a metal superstructure with glass tiles that are sturdy enough to endure unexpected weather events like storms. When built with a commercial goal in mind, these superstructures include advanced technology, including climate control, humidifiers, cooling fans, atomizers, and mist sprayers, all connected to a computer-assisted system. This technology monitors the crops 24 hours a day, seven days a week, and automatically changes the conditions to safeguard the crops from harm. Some greenhouses also have multiple climatic conditions favorable for multiple crops under a single roof.

Plants grown in greenhouses often require extra care. For example, they need watering more often than plants grown outdoors because the warm, humid conditions inside a greenhouse cause water to evaporate quickly. Plants also need to be fertilized more frequently in a greenhouse. One of the most important benefits of the glasshouse is that it restricts pest attacks.

## The Science behind Greenhouses

Many are intrigued about how a clear glass-walled house produces more plants, especially in harsh conditions. Many might even think it's a pretty way to showcase a farm. However, you'll be surprised how basic the working mechanism of a greenhouse is.

It all starts and ends with the sunlight and warmth it gives to the crops. As we know, the primary function of a greenhouse is to maintain a favorable climatic condition for crops and preserve energy inside for longer. This is possible when the glass allows solar radiation to form visible sunlight into the structure. Solar radiation is absorbed by plants, surfaces, and other objects present in the greenhouse and is converted to heat energy. Plants and other objects emit heat energy, and the greenhouse traps that energy inside the superstructure, preventing it from dissipating to the outside atmosphere. The glass acts as an insulator allowing visible sunlight to enter but doesn't allow the heat emitted to escape the greenhouse. The accumulation of heat via convection in the greenhouse makes it warmer, raising the temperature inside the building. This complete process is known as the greenhouse effect.

Apart from the mechanism explained above, many factors enhance the functioning of a greenhouse. From passive heating systems to ventilation, it is imperative to understand the science behind them and how they are essential in modern-day greenhouse farming.

- **Air Circulation**

In a traditional house, warm air rises to the top and is replaced by cooler air from outside through windows. However, the warm air is trapped inside a greenhouse, causing the temperature to rise. Greenhouses rely on air circulation to prevent the temperature from becoming too hot and damaging crops. Air circulation occurs when warm air rises to the top of the greenhouse and is blown out through vents or pushed by powerful fans. It allows cooler air to enter the bottom of the greenhouse, creating a circulating effect. In addition to regulating temperature, air circulation helps evenly distribute humidity and CO2 levels throughout the greenhouse. As a result, it plays a vital role in maintaining optimal growing conditions for plants.

- **Passive Heating**

The greenhouse might not get direct sunlight due to heavy rains or even hazy, cloudy weather at a certain time. These instances can deteriorate the produce grown inside as it is hard to sustain the warm temperature inside, so passive heating is used. Passive heating is heating your greenhouse without using any external energy source. Standard greenhouses rely on the sun or fossil fuels to heat the air inside, but passive heating harnesses the power of the Earth to warm the greenhouse. There are a few different ways to do this, but the most common is to use a buried water line. Water is an excellent conductor of heat, so burying a water pipe in the ground next to the greenhouse transfers heat from the Earth into the water. The water circulates through the greenhouse, warming the air inside. Another common method is to install a concrete floor; concrete absorbs heat during the day and releases it at night, providing a steady source of warm air for your plants.

- **Artificial Lighting**

Artificial lighting is often used in greenhouses when natural sunlight is insufficient, when plants need extra light during the winter, or to promote plant growth at night. This method uses grow lights that impart light close to the sun's spectrum. Many grow lights are tailored and made according to the specific plant's requirements. When choosing artificial lighting for a greenhouse, it is important to consider the plants grown inside the space. For example, succulent plants require less light than leafy greens. In addition, the greenhouse size and the distance between the plants also affect the amount of light needed. After considering these factors, you can determine how many hours of artificial light are needed each day and what bulbs will work best.

- **Carbon Dioxide Enrichment**

Carbon dioxide is one of the essential nutrients for plant growth. Carbon dioxide enrichment inside a greenhouse helps boost plant growth by increasing the amount of available carbon dioxide for photosynthesis. Intelligent sensors supply liquid carbon dioxide.

They are used to fulfill any shortcoming in the amount of gas in the greenhouse. However, it is important to maintain safe carbon dioxide levels to avoid damaging or killing plants.

## The Difference between Traditional Farming and Green House

Traditional farming in today's world has a diminishing impact. The evolution of modern farming technologies has pushed farming horizons to new limits. At the same time, global climate crises like water shortages, global warming, uneven climate changes, and pest attacks have forced farmers to consider new farming methods immune to these problems. A greenhouse is one of the novel farming techniques farmers use to tackle a global problem. Here are key differences between traditional on-field farming and greenhouse farming.

Greenhouse farming allows you to control the environment where your plants grow, giving you greater control over temperature, humidity, and ventilation, leading to higher yields and healthier plants. However, greenhouses are expensive to set up. Traditional on-the-field farming doesn't allow you to control the growing environment, but it's less expensive and easier to set up. On the downside, yield may suffer due to pests, weather, and soil quality.

Traditional farming is growing crops in open fields, meaning plants are subject to whatever weather conditions happen to be present during the growing season. While this sometimes results in lower-quality plants, farmers deal with fewer pests and diseases. Greenhouses are compact and can produce similar crops, which would normally take acres of land to produce. Greenhouses can be located closer to population centers as they are not subject to the same space limitations as traditional farms resulting in fresher produce for consumers and fewer transportation costs. They also produce higher crop yields than traditional farming resulting in more profits for farmers.

## How to Build a Greenhouse

To build a greenhouse, you need to consider many factors. From the size of the greenhouse to the technology needed to run it. Here is a simple guide on how to build a greenhouse.

### *Choose a Location*

Before building a greenhouse, choosing the right location is important. Evaluate the sunlight the location gets throughout the day. Experts recommend building a greenhouse facing in the north direction to maximize the sun exposure. It is also essential to ensure the location is fairly level so that your greenhouse doesn't have any drainage issues. There should be a source of electricity nearby for smooth appliance operations. Consider a location protected from strong winds and is a good drainage site.

### *Choose a Structure*

Once you have chosen the right location for a greenhouse, the next step is choosing the right structure. The size of your greenhouse depends on the scale of farming you wish to operate. The ideal dimension is 8 feet by 10 feet for a backyard greenhouse for gardening or self-sustenance farming. Farmers looking for commercial farming should aim to build 20 feet by 30 feet structures.

Choosing the right structure and frame type is as important as selecting the greenhouse material. The frame significantly affects how well your greenhouse will withstand the elements and resist moisture damage. Consider the climate conditions. If you live in an area with high winds, choosing a metallic frame that can withstand gusts without collapsing is crucial. Aluminum frames are a good option in hot climates because they won't warp or corrode. If you plan on growing taller plants, you'll need a taller frame to give them plenty of headroom. Also, use any lumber type, but it is recommended to use pressure-treated or rot-resistant. These types help extend your greenhouse's life and save you money in the long run. Once you have your lumber, cut it to size and assemble it using nails or screws. Make sure the frame is level and square before adding the walls and roof. Based on frame requirements, there are two structure types.

- **Lean on Structure**

Building a lean-to structure is much easier than attaching the greenhouse to an existing structure. A lean-to provides much-needed stability during high winds and heavy snowfalls. It's important to choose a spot that gets plenty of sun and has good drainage. Select the material for the frame - metal is a popular choice because it's strong and durable, but wood can also be used. Once you have the materials, it's time to start assembly. If you're not comfortable working with tools, plenty of kits include everything you need to get the job done.

- **Quonset Frames**

Quonset frames are made of steel and are very strong. They're also relatively easy to assemble, making them a good choice for do-it-yourselfers. You'll need to purchase the steel rods and fittings and cut them to size. Once you have all of your supplies, you can build the frame. Quonset frames are typically held together with bolts and nuts, so it's important to ensure that everything is tight before moving on. If everything is done correctly, your frame will be strong and stable - perfect for supporting a greenhouse.

### *Choose a Foundation*

There are three main greenhouse foundations: gravel, wooden, and concrete. Each has its benefits and drawbacks. Gravel is the most common foundation as it's relatively inexpensive and easy to install. However, it is difficult to keep weeds from growing in the gravel, and it doesn't provide much insulation against heat or cold. Wooden foundations are more expensive than gravel but easier to keep clean and provide good insulation. The downside is that they're vulnerable to rot and termites. Concrete is the most durable foundation option, but it's also the most expensive. It's important to consult with an expert before choosing a foundation for your greenhouse. With the right foundation in place, you'll be well on your way to creating a beautiful and productive space for your plants.

*Choose a Glass or Covering*

Greenhouses provide an optimal environment for year-round plant growth, but only if made with the right materials. One of the most important choices you'll make when building a greenhouse is the glass you use. There are three main greenhouse glass types: toughened, laminated, and polycarbonate, and each has its advantages. Toughened glass is the strongest option and ideal for greenhouses in exposed locations. Laminated glass is two layers of glass bonded with a plastic interlayer, making it more impact-resistant than regular glass. Polycarbonate is a lightweight plastic that's shatterproof and offers excellent heat insulation.

If your main intention is to use your greenhouse as a hobby or self-gardening, it is recommended to use covering like polyethylene rather than glass. Polyethylene is one of the most popular choices because it's lightweight and inexpensive. However, it isn't very durable and must be replaced more frequently than other materials. Once your glass or covering is selected, mindfully apply them, complimenting the outer frame. Leave space open for vents on the roof and the door on the structure's base.

## Supplement with Necessary Technology

Adding various farming technology is the last piece of the puzzle once your structure is ready with the glass fitted. Are you undecided about what technology you need to install in your greenhouse? After all, you want to ensure your plants get the best possible care, meaning having the right tools for the job. Here are a few technology systems useful in a greenhouse:

- **A Water Filtration System**: Helps ensure your plants get clean water, free of any harmful chemicals or pollutants.

- **An Automated Watering System:** This is a great way to save time and keep your plants watered regularly.

- **Grow Lights:** These are a great way to supplement light during the night or when sunlight exposure is minimal.

- **Ventilation Fans:** Help regulate temperature and humidity levels in the greenhouse, keeping your plants healthy and happy.

- **Thermostat:** This device automatically increases and decreases temperatures in the farming space, providing crops with favorable climatic conditions.

- **Vents:** Vents help regulate the temperature inside the greenhouse, keeping it consistent during the day and night. In addition, vents help keep the humidity levels low, preventing condensation and mold growth. Greenhouses get hot, stuffy, and unhealthy places for plants to grow without vents.

Installing some or all of these technology systems in your greenhouse gives your plants the best possible chance of thriving.

Assembling all the components can take time, so it's best to use professional assistance, especially if you are building a big greenhouse.

**Plants Grown in a Greenhouse**

Here are a few examples of plants ideal for growing in your greenhouse. These plants are easily monitored, high yielding, and packed with healthy nutrients.

## 1.  Cucumbers

Cucumbers are a refreshing and versatile vegetable enjoyed in a variety of dishes. They are also relatively easy to grow, making them ideal for greenhouse gardening. Cucumbers require full sun and well-drained soil to prosper and watered regularly. They can be harvested in 75 days, ideal for commercial farming.

## 2.  Broccoli

You might not think of broccoli as the most exciting vegetable, but it is an ideal candidate for greenhouse farming. Broccoli is a cool-weather crop grown year-round in most climates. They can be harvested in just 60-90 days and are highly nutritious vegetables packed with vitamins and minerals. Broccoli is a pest-resistant crop, so you won't have to worry about dealing with pesky insects.

## 3.  Carrots

When planting carrots in your greenhouse, you must choose the right carrot seeds for your climate. Plant the seeds in small pots or trays inside your greenhouse. Carrots need full sun and well-drained soil to grow properly, so give them plenty of watering regularly about twice a week and fertilizing them every month.

## 4. Lettuce

Lettuce can be grown from seed and doesn't require much space or care. In addition, lettuce is a cool-weather crop, so it is grown year-round in a greenhouse. Lettuce is also relatively pest-resistant, so you don't have to worry about insect damage. Last but not least, lettuce is packed with nutrients and a great source of vitamins A and C, folic acid, and iron.

## 5. Tomatoes

Tomatoes love lots of sun, so the more sun they get, the better. They need an ideal growing condition of 25-27 degrees C and are not water-intensive crops. However, tomatoes need a fair amount of care as they're notoriously picky and don't taste as good as when picked before they're ripe.

## 6. Microgreens

Microgreens are one of the ideal vegetables grown in a greenhouse for several reasons. They are incredibly easy and quick to grow, often taking as little as two weeks from seed to harvest. Microgreens are widely used in various dishes, from salads to soups to sandwiches. They also pack a serious nutritional punch, loaded with vitamins, minerals, and antioxidants. Lastly, microgreens are relatively inexpensive to grow, making them a great option for home gardeners and commercial farmers.

## 7. Bell peppers

Bell peppers need warm, humid conditions, are grown year-round in most climates, and require little attention once planted. Water your bell peppers regularly and fertilize them every few weeks to ensure a bountiful crop.

## 8. Ornamental Plants

Ornamental plants are a versatile, easy-to-grow option that will add color and life to your space. These lovely plants are beautiful and packed with nutrients. Compared to other vegetables, they have a high commercial value and are relatively easy to care for, making them great for beginner gardeners. Create a well-draining soil mix by combining equal parts peat moss, perlite, and compost in pots or stacks to ensure healthy growth and bountiful blooms. These plants need medium sunlight and hydration and are not work extensive plants.

So, there you have everything you need to know about greenhouses. Greenhouses are an excellent way to extend your growing season and protect your plants from bad weather. They are also used to create ideal growing conditions for delicate plants. However, before you build a greenhouse, it's important to research and ensure you have the right location and materials.

# Chapter 9

# More Off-the-Grid Projects

You've decided to go off the grid. You're tired of being tied to a job you hate, tired of the rat race and the never-ending cycle of working to pay bills. You're ready to simplify your life and live off-the-grid, closer to nature. But, before you take the plunge, there are a few things you need to consider. One of the most important things to consider is how you will support yourself financially. Starting a business is a great way but choosing the right businesses for your off-the-grid lifestyle is important. Here are a few ideas to get you started.

## Soap Making

Living off the grid is challenging, but it doesn't mean you have to go without creature comforts. Many people living off the grid are finding creative ways to generate revenue. Soap-making is a promising endeavor. By producing all-natural, handmade soap, you can support yourself financially and tap into a growing market for artisanal products.

## *The Soap Making Process*

- The first step is to assemble the right ingredients. You'll need fat or oil, lye, water, fresh flowers and plants, and optional scent or colorants. You can use any animal or vegetable product for the fat or oil, including tallow, lard, olive oil, coconut oil, etc. The lye must be food grade and can be purchased online or at hardware stores. Use distilled or rainwater.

- Next, you need to render the fat or oil, meaning melting it down so that it's in a liquid form. You can use a solar dehydrator or a solar oven to melt the oil. If you're using solid fats like tallow or lard, you'll need to do this over low heat. After the fat has melted completely, allow it to cool. Measure out the required lye and slowly add it to the fat, stirring constantly.

- Now it's time to mix the lye and fat mixture, known as "saponification." This can be done by hand with a large spoon or mixer. If you're using a blender, start on low speed and slowly increase to avoid splattering. The mixture will become thick and creamy as it saponifies.

- Once the mixture has saponified, add the water (again, slowly) and mix well. At this point, you can add any flower petals or herbs from your farm or use essential oils or other scents or colorants if desired. Finally, pour the soap into molds and allow it to harden for 24-48 hours. Once it's hardened, remove it from the mold and cut it into bars. Allow the bars to cure for 4-6 weeks in a cool, dark place before using.

## *Why Make Soap at Home?*

There are multiple reasons to make soap at home. Perhaps you want a more natural alternative to store-bought soap. Or maybe you're interested in saving money. But one of the biggest reasons is tapping the natural cosmetic industry and earning revenue. Here are some reasons making natural handmade soap at your off-the-grid home can become a great enterprise.

1.  **You Choose Your Ingredients:** Most store-bought soaps contain harsh chemicals that dry your skin, but when you make soap at home, you use all-natural ingredients sourced from your farm and gentle on your skin. In addition, making soap is a great way to recycle used cooking oil, which would otherwise be disposed of in a landfill. Using ingredients straight from your farm produce and waste

enables you to spend much less on raw materials saving a huge investment.

2. **You Save Money:** Store-bought soap is expensive, and homemade soap often costs much less. In addition, making soap is a great way to use leftover ingredients that you might otherwise throw away. For example, add used coffee grounds, oatmeal, or shredded paper to your soap to give it exfoliating properties.

3. **You Make a Profit:** If you enjoy making soap and have extra time on your hands, sell your soap to friends, family, and neighbors. Homemade soap makes a great gift, and many people are willing to pay premium prices for unique, handcrafted items. You can also sell your soap at farmer's markets, craft fairs, and online.

## Candle-Making

Making candles at home is a great way to earn money and be self-sufficient. Candles are relatively easy to make, and the materials are readily available. In addition, making candles is a great way to reuse old candle stubs and scraps of wax. Use a high-quality wax and fragrance oil for the best results.

### *Materials and Equipment Needed*

To get started, you need a few supplies. First, you'll need wax. Some of the popular choices are tallow, soy wax, and beeswax. You'll also need natural fragrance oil, flower petals, wicks, and candle molds. You can find these supplies at your local craft store or online.

### *The Candle-Making Process*

- **Choose the Wax You'd Like to Use:** Source tallow or animal wax, soy wax, or beeswax to produce all-natural candles. Some considerations include the scent of your candles and the hardness or softness levels you prefer.

- **Melt the Wax:** This is done in a double boiler or a makeshift one by placing a metal bowl on top of a pot of boiling water using solar energy. Slowly melt the wax, occasionally stirring, until it is completely liquid.

- **Add Your Fragrance:** Add essential oils, herbs like jasmine, chamomile flowers, etc., and spices like cinnamon and nutmeg, and stir well to combine.

- **Fix the Wick:** Before pouring in the wax, ensure the wick is fixed to the bottom of the container. Dip the wick in the melting wax and immediately glue it to the bottom of the container to secure it. Allow the wax to solidify for five minutes.

- **Pour the Wax into Your Mold**: Be careful not to pour too quickly or when it is too hot, as this can cause air bubbles to form in your candles. Fill the mold to just below the tip so there is room for the wick.

- **Allow the Wax to Cool and Harden**: Depending on the wax you're using, this procedure might take several hours. Once the wax is hard, move on to the next step.

- **Trim the Wick:** Cut the wick about 1/4 inch shorter than the height of your candle. This will help prevent it from smoking when lit.

### *Why Make Candles at Home?*

Candles are a wonderful way to add ambiance to any setting and make great gifts. These products are used in spa centers and meditation retreats and are a hit among anyone who wants to relax, so there is a huge market for essential oil candles. The truth is that homemade candles have significant advantages over store-bought varieties. Here are some reasons to make your candles:

1. **Cheaper to Make**: Candles are expensive, especially if you buy them from a high-end store. But when you make candles sourced from your farm, you save a lot of money. The cost of wax and fragrance oil is relatively low, and you can reuse old candle stubs to make new candles.

2. **Better for the Environment:** Most store-bought candles are made with paraffin wax, a petroleum product. When burned, paraffin candles release harmful toxins into the air. But when you make candles at home, you use eco-friendly materials like soy wax or beeswax.

3. **Money Generating Source**: These homemade candles are more creative and personal, attracting much online clientele.

You can make them in different colors, fragrances, and sizes and even add special embellishments like beads or shells. Natural fragrance candles are highly demanded in the aromatherapy industry and mediation retreats. Sell them on Instagram, an e-commerce platform, or any farmer's market. It's sure to attract a lot of clients.

## Basketry

Basketry is an ancient art practiced around the world for centuries. Baskets are traditionally made from natural materials like wood, reeds, and grasses, which are easily accessible and sustainable. The basket-making process is therapeutic and meditative, and the finished product is beautiful and functional and can generate good revenue.

### *Materials and Equipment Needed*

The material you use for your basket depends on the basket you want to make. For example, wicker baskets are typically made from willow branches, while reed baskets are made from, you guessed it, reeds. Other popular materials include grasses, bamboo, and even paper. You'll need a few basic tools to get started; a sharp knife and a pair of scissors are always helpful. You'll also need something to weave the material, like strips of cloth or raffia. If you're using willow branches, you'll need a couple of additional supplies: a saw to cut the branches and a spindle to strip the bark.

### *The Basket-Making Process*

Basket making is a great way to use up any extra materials you have lying around on your off-the-grid farm, and the result is beautiful and functional. Here are the basic steps for making a simple basket:

- **Gather Your Materials:** The first step is to gather all the materials you'll need for your basket. For the basket's body, use any reed or grass; for the rim, some sturdy twine; and for the handle, use more twine or a strip of bark from a tree.

- **Soak Your Reeds:** Once all your materials are gathered, it's time to soak the reeds or grass for the basket's body. Soaking makes them pliable and easier to work with. Simply place them in a bucket of water and let them soak for at least an hour.

- **Start Weaving:** Now it's time to start weaving your basket. Take two soaked reeds and tie them together at one end. Then, weave them in and out of each other, keeping the weave tight. As you add more reeds, continue weaving them in and out, always keeping the weave tight.

- **Finish the Rim:** Once you've reached the desired width for your basket, it's time to finish the rim. Take a length of twine and tie it around the outside of the basket, making sure to pull it tight. Then, trim off any excess twine.

- **Adding the Finishing Touches:** The final step is to add any finishing touches you desire. These could include adding a handle, decorating the basket with beads or shells, or varnishing it to protect it from the elements.

### *Why Make Baskets at Home?*

Basket making is a great way to express your creativity, and the finished product is practical and beautiful. Best of all, you don't need special skills or materials to start. All you need is a bit of patience and a few basic supplies. Here are a few reasons we think you should try basketry.

1. **It's Inexpensive**: You often find the supplies you need for free or very cheap. For example, willow branches grow near rivers or streams. If you want to get creative, use recycled materials like old clothes or newspapers.

2. **Generate Revenue:** There are many ways to sell your baskets, like local craft fairs or online. You can also set up a website to sell your baskets. Whichever way you sell your baskets, ensure you price them correctly. Basket prices vary depending on the size, design, and materials.

### Flower Arrangement

Flower arranging is another great way to spruce up your home and add a personal touch. The best part about flower arranging is using flowers from your off-the-grid garden. While many people think of flower arranging as a simple way to decorate a room, the truth is that it is a truly rewarding business. It gives you a chance to express your creativity, but it also allows you to connect with various clientele personally.

### *Materials and Equipment Needed*

If you're thinking of trying your hand at flower arranging, there are a few basic supplies you'll need to get started. You'll need a container to hold your arrangement. A vase or basket will work fine, but you can also get creative and use an interesting bowl or pitcher. You'll also need something to use as filler material; this is anything from rocks or stones to moss or leaves.

Once you have your filler material, it's time to choose your flowers. Start growing a range of flowers on your farm from focal flowers, which will be the centerpieces of your arrangement, and filler flowers to help fill in space and add color. When choosing your flowers, it's important to consider the color and the shape of the blooms.

### *The Flower Arranging Process*

Now that you have all the supplies you need, it's time to get started. While there are no hard-and-fast rules to flower arranging, a basic process will help you create beautiful arrangements every time.

- **Start with the Filler Material:** Begin by adding your filler material to the bottom of your container. This supports the stems of your flowers and keeps them in place.

- **Cut the Stems:** Once you're happy with the selection of your flowers, it's time to cut the stems. Cut the stems at an angle using sharp scissors or shears; it helps the flowers absorb more water and stay fresh longer.

- **Add the Filler Flowers:** Next, add the filler flowers to the arrangement. These can be smaller blooms or buds that will add color and texture to your design.

- **Add the Focal Flowers:** The focal flowers should be the stars of your arrangement, so add them last. Choose blooms of different sizes and shapes to create an interesting design.

- **Add Water:** Finally, add water to the container and enjoy your beautiful flower arrangement.

### *What Makes Flower Arranging So Rewarding?*

There are many reasons flower arranging is such a rewarding experience. For some, it's a way to express their creativity. Others see it as a way to connect with nature. From a business point of view, flower arranging is a thriving business, especially in the events sector like weddings, funerals, parties, etc. Here are a few advantages of a flower-arranging business.

- **Connects You with Nature:** For many people, flower arranging is a way to connect with nature. If you love spending time outdoors, working with flowers is a great way to bring a piece of nature into your home.

- **It's a Profitable Skill:** Flower arranging is a great option if you want to make some extra money. While you won't get rich quick, you can make a decent income from selling your arrangements if you're good at it. You can also use your skills to decorate weddings, parties, and other events. Market your business so people know where to find you and what services you offer - create a website, hand out business cards, and advertise in local publications.

## Natural Dyes

If you're interested in exploring the world of natural dyes, there are a few things you need to know before you get started. First, natural dyes are not as color-fast as synthetic dyes, meaning they will fade over time. Hence, it's vital to consider this when choosing fabric or other materials to dye.

Second, natural dyes can be made from various materials, including leaves, bark, and flowers. You can even use food waste, like coffee grounds or avocado pits. The possibilities are endless, so get creative and experiment with different materials.

Third, natural dyes will produce a range of colors, from light pastels to deep, rich hues. The color of the dye depends on the materials you use and the length of time you allow the fabric to soak in the dye bath.

Lastly, natural dyes will not produce an exact color match every time. This is part of the beauty of natural dyes, so embrace the imperfections and enjoy the process.

### *Materials and Equipment Needed*

To get started, you'll need a few supplies. You'll need some fabric or other material to dye; cotton, linen, and silk are all good choices.

You'll also need a dye bath, which can be made from many materials like plant material, such as leaves or bark. You'll also need a mordant in addition to your dye bath. A mordant is a chemical that aids the adhesion of the dye to the cloth. Common mordants include alum and vinegar. Lastly, you'll need a pot to boil your dye bath, gloves, and old clothes you don't mind getting stained.

### *The Dye-Making Process*

Now that you have all the necessary supplies, it's time to start making natural dyes. Here is a step-by-step guide to help you get started.

- **Prepare Your Dye Bath**: Begin by adding your plant material to a pot of water. If you're using leaves or bark, you'll need to add more material to the dye bath to create a rich color.

- **Boil the Dye Bath:** Place the pot of dye bath on the stove and bring it to a boil. Allow the dye bath to boil for at least 30 minutes.

- **Add the Mordant:** Once the dye bath has boiled, add the mordant and stir to combine.

- **Add the Fabric:** Carefully add your fabric to the dye bath and allow it to soak for at least an hour. The longer you allow the fabric to soak, the deeper the color.

- **Remove the Fabric:** Once the fabric has reached the desired color, carefully remove it from the dye bath and rinse it in cold water.

- **Hang the Fabric to Dry:** Hang the fabric to dry in a well-ventilated area. Once it's dry, you can enjoy your beautiful, naturally dyed fabric.

### *What Makes Dying Business Rewarding?*

There is a growing demand for handmade goods today, and natural dyes are no exception. By turning your farm into dye works, you can create beautiful hand-dyed fabrics people will be happy to pay for. This will provide you with a steady income, but it also allows you to live a more sustainable lifestyle.

## Quilt making

Few things are as cozy as a handmade quilt on a cold winter's night. Quilts have been around for centuries, and the art of quilt making is still practiced today. Many different techniques are used to create a quilt, from traditional piecing to modern applique. The choices of using organic fabrics grown in-house on your farm will result in an organic homemade quilt of the highest quality.

Quilt making is a rewarding hobby enjoyed by people of all ages. Whether you're only getting started or an experienced quilter, there's always something new to learn. The best part about quilt making is that you can make money selling your quilts.

*Materials and Equipment Needed*

You'll need a few supplies to get started in quilt making. You'll need fabric - quilting fabric is sold by the yard and found in various colors and patterns. You need batting, a cotton or wool filling between the fabric layers and is sourced from the farm or brought from a farmer's market. You'll also need a sewing machine, thread, scissors, and a rotary cutter. A rotary cutter is a handheld tool that makes it easy to cut the fabric into straight strips.

*The Quilt Making Process*

Follow these steps to create a simple quilt top.

- **Cut the Fabric:** Cut your fabric into strips. If you're using a rotary cutter, use a self-healing cutting mat to protect your surfaces.

- **Sew the Strips Together:** Once the strips are cut, it's time to sew them together. Sew the strips together side by side, making sure to line up the edges. You will use a sewing machine to do this.

- **Press the Seams:** Once all the strips are sewn together, press the seams with an iron. This helps the quilt lie flat when it's finished.

- **Layer the Fabric:** Now it's time to layer the quilt top, batting, and backing fabric.

- **Quilt the Layers Together:** Once the layers are aligned, quilt them together by hand or machine. If you're quilting by machine, use a walking foot to prevent the fabric from bunching.

- **Bind the Quilt:** To finish the quilt, you bind the edges, which is done by hand or machine. If you're binding by machine, use a zigzag stitch to prevent the fabric from fraying.

- **Wash the Quilt:** Wash it in cold water once it is finished. This will help the quilt lie flat and prevent the fabric from bleeding.

### *What makes Quilting Rewarding?*

If you're living off the grid, you probably have a lot of natural resources at your disposal. With a little creativity, you can turn quilt-making into a profitable business. Use scraps of fabric from previous projects to create new quilts. This is a fantastic method to reuse items while saving money on supplies. Collect plants and flowers from your surroundings to decorate your quilts. Not only will this add a unique touch to your products, but it will also save you money buying embellishments.

If you have access to sheep or other animals, consider using their wool to make your quilts. It will give your quilts a rustic look and feel and will be a great way to support local farmers.

Use natural dyes to give your quilts unique colors and a great way to add value to your products and stand out from the competition. You can easily turn quilt making into a profitable business with a little effort by using natural resources and being creative with your designs.

When you live off-the-grid, it is important to find ways to earn money and become financially self-sufficient, and these businesses help you achieve that. If you are creative and have an entrepreneurial spirit, these opportunities will help you earn money and become financially self-sufficient when living off the grid.

# Conclusion

While forsaking tap water, ready-to-use power outlets, and store-bought foods may prove challenging, you'll quickly realize how liberating an off-the-grid lifestyle can be. You will no longer be consumed by the uncertainty of the world, rampant inflation, high-priced utilities, or buying everyday products that you could perfectly make on your own. In short, off-grid projects grant you the independence to live a life that resonates with your own habits, beliefs, and convictions.

Going off-grid has considerable advantages: autonomy, self-sufficiency, financial freedom, and a more harmonious relationship with nature. Whether you plan to go full-out or simply try a few DIY projects to set yourself out on that path, this lifestyle change is guaranteed to save and teach you plenty in the long run.

As we've seen, rain barrels are ideal for collecting water and irrigation when it comes to your everyday needs. In parallel, remember that operating solar or wind power requires plenty of preparation before you can begin generating your own electricity. Be sure to follow the provided step-by-step instructions and safety precautions for each of these projects. The same goes for raising chickens, collecting eggs, farming bees, and growing fruit, vegetables, herbs, and grains for your home garden. Also, dig deeper into greenhouses to see if they'd be a good fit for your environment. All this shows you must cover your basis and not leave anything to chance – the better prepared you are, the better equipped you will be at managing emergency or survival situations.

Hopefully, all the knowledge, techniques, and DIY projects compiled in this insightful book will have effectively prepared you for an off-the-grid lifestyle. While it can take a few days or weeks to fully adjust, the sense of security and self-support you stand to gain in the end will be well worth the effort. You never know when these newly acquired skills and trades will come in handy. On that note, be safe, stay sharp, and good luck!

Thank you for buying and reading/listening to our book. If you found this book useful/helpful please take a few minutes and leave a review on Amazon.com or Audible.com (if you bought the audio version).

# References

Greenwood, J. (n.d.). What is water recycling, and why is it important? Wcs-Group.Co.Uk. https://www.wcs-group.co.uk/wcs-blog/what-is-water-recycling

CDC. (2021, May 16). Benefits of healthy eating. Centers for Disease Control and Prevention. https://www.cdc.gov/nutrition/resources-publications/benefits-of-healthy-eating.html

Off-Grid Energy. (2020, February 6). The pros and cons of going off the grid. Off-Grid Energy Australia. https://www.offgridenergy.com.au/the-pros-and-cons-of-going-off-the-grid/

» M. A. M. (2010, July 13). Solar lawn mower! Instructables. https://www.instructables.com/Solar-Lawn-Mower-1

Arcuri, L. (2010, July 8). A beginner's guide to beekeeping. The Spruce. https://www.thespruce.com/beginners-guide-to-beekeeping-3016857

Beekeeping 101: Harvesting honey. (n.d.). Almanac.Com https://www.almanac.com/beekeeping-101-collecting-honey

Choosing a beehive: Buy or build? (n.d.). Parisfarmersunion.Com. http://blog.parisfarmersunion.com/2016/04/choosing-beehive-buy-or-build.html?m=1

Cindy, M. (2020, February 19). 6 tips for building a solar-powered greenhouse in your garden. The Herb Cottage. https://www.theherbcottage.com/6-tips-for-building-a-solar-powered-greenhouse-in-your-garden/

Differences between wind power and solar energy. (n.d.). Directenergy.Com https://www.directenergy.com/learning-center/differences-between-wind-solar-energy

» M. A. M. (2010, July 13). Solar lawn mower! Instructables. https://www.instructables.com/Solar-Lawn-Mower-1/

Arcuri, L. (2010, July 8). A beginner's guide to beekeeping. The Spruce. https://www.thespruce.com/beginners-guide-to-beekeeping-3016857

Beekeeping 101: Harvesting honey. (n.d.). Almanac.Com. https://www.almanac.com/beekeeping-101-collecting-honey

Browning, A. (2021, April 21). How to make Natural Dyes from Food (Step by step guide). FiberArtsy.Com; Annette Browning. https://www.fiberartsy.com/how-to-make-natural-dyes-from-food/

Carolynn. (2013, March 9). Survival candle-making 101. Off The Grid News. https://www.offthegridnews.com/current-events/top-headlines/survival-candle-making-101/

Choosing a beehive: Buy or build? (n.d.). Parisfarmersunion.Com.
    http://blog.parisfarmersunion.com/2016/04/choosing-
    beehive-buy-or-build.html?m=1

Cindy, M. (2020, February 19). 6 tips for building a solar-powered
    greenhouse in your garden. The Herb Cottage.
    https://www.theherbcottage.com/6-tips-for-building-a-solar-
    powered-greenhouse-in-your-garden/

Differences between wind power and solar energy. (n.d.).
    Directenergy.Com. https://www.directenergy.com/learning-
    center/differences-between-wind-solar-energy

Donations-Kiva. (2012, April 25). The perfect beginner's guide to
    off-grid living. Workaway Blog.
    https://www.workaway.info/en/stories/5-reasons-off-grid-
    living-workaway

Esther. (2012, February 18). How to make your own soap. Off The
    Grid News. https://www.offthegridnews.com/current-
    events/top-headlines/how-to-make-your-own-soap/

Garman, J. (2019, February 1). How to start beekeeping in your
    backyard. Backyard Beekeeping.
    https://backyardbeekeeping.iamcountryside.com/beekeeping
    -101/how-to-start-a-honey-bee-farm/

Green City Growers. (2017, March 30). Green City growers.
    Greencitygrowers.Com; Green City Growers, LLC.
    https://greencitygrowers.com/blog/10-reasons-to-grow-
    your-own-food/

How do solar panels work? The science of solar explained. (2016, March 15). Select Energy. https://solect.com/the-science-of-solar-how-solar-panels-work/

How does solar work? (n.d.). Energy.Gov https://www.energy.gov/eere/solar/how-does-solar-work

How to start beekeeping (A complete guide). (2021, June 29). Beekeeping For Newbies. https://www.beekeepingfornewbies.com/how-to-start-beekeeping/

Hyder, Z. (2019, November 29). Off-grid solar systems: An introductory guide. Solar Reviews. https://www.solarreviews.com/blog/off-grid-solar-systems

Installing and maintaining a small wind electric system. (n.d.). Energy.Gov. from https://www.energy.gov/energysaver/installing-and-maintaining-small-wind-electric-system

Inverter/chargers and charge controllers: Do you need both? (n.d.). Magnum-Dimensions.Com. https://www.magnum-dimensions.com/knowledge/pvstorage/inverterchargers-and-charge-controllers-do-you-need-both

Joan, B. (2012, April 25). Difference Between Wind Power and solar power. Differencebetween.Net; Difference Between. http://www.differencebetween.net/science/physics-science/difference-between-wind-power-and-solar-power/

Kearney, H. (2020, June 23). Protect your bees from hot weather.
Keeping Backyard Bees.
https://www.keepingbackyardbees.com/protect-your-bees-
in-hot-weather-zbwz1807zsau/

Krane, J., & Bennett, J. (2018, November 6). 8 simple steps to
arrange flowers like a pro. Better Homes & Gardens.
https://www.bhg.com/decorating/home-accessories/flower-
arranging/how-to-make-a-flower-arrangement/

Kunz, N. (2020, December 1). How to find the best solar panels in
the UK (cost & efficiency guide 2021).

Light, D. (2019, March 12). Benefits of the off-grid solar system
[infographic]. Dlight.Com; d.light.
https://www.dlight.com/blog/benefits-of-off-grid-solar-
system-infographic/

Max. (2021, December 16). Difference between solar energy and
wind energy. Industrial Manufacturing Blog | Linquip.
https://www.linquip.com/blog/difference-between-solar-
energy-and-wind-energy/

May, R. (2014, September 12). How to make a quilt in six steps.
Mother Earth News – The Original Guide To Living
Wisely; Mother Earth News.
https://www.motherearthnews.com/diy/how-to-make-a-
quilt-ze0z1409zcwil/

Pieper, A. (2019, August 12). 6 common bee predators and how to
protect your hive. MorningChores.
https://morningchores.com/bee-predators/

Projects. (n.d.). Windpower Engineering & Development. https://www.windpowerengineering.com/category/projects/

Waterworth, K. (2013, October 9). Growing plants in A greenhouse - suitable plants for greenhouse gardening. Gardening Know-How. https://www.gardeningknowhow.com/special/greenhouses/plants-for-greenhouses.htm

What are solar cells? (including types, efficiency, and developments). (n.d.). Twi-Global.Com. https://www.twi-global.com/technical-knowledge/faqs/what-are-solar-cells

What does off the grid mean, and how to live off the grid? (n.d.). Enel X. https://corporate.enelx.com/en/question-and-answers/what-does-off-the-grid-mean

What types of solar panels are there? (mono- and polycrystalline explained). (2021, July 5).

Wilson, K. (n.d.). How to build A solar panel from scratch. Those Solar Guys. https://thosesolarguys.com/how-to-build-a-solar-panel-from-scratch/

(N.d.-a). Renewableenergyhub.Co.Uk. https://www.renewableenergyhub.co.uk/main/solar-panels/types-of-solar-cell/

(N.d.-b). Wthitv.Com. https://www.wthitv.com/archive/how-to-protect-bees-during-the-winter/article_22fd0b16-4953-5752-a506-3532ebc5a288.html

Eric. (2016, August 10). Grow your own food with an off-grid farm in a box. Off-Grid World. https://offgridworld.com/grow-your-own-food-with-an-off-grid-farm-in-a-box/

Geror, L. (2020, May 3). The what and why of hydroponic farming. Vertical Roots. https://www.verticalroots.com/the-what-and-why-of-hydroponic-farming/

Huffstetler, E. (2012, March 20). The best vegetables to grow in small gardens. The Spruce. https://www.thespruce.com/high-yield-vegetable-plants-for-small-garden-spaces-1388683

Jabbour, N. (2020, May 15). Kitchen garden basics: How to start growing food today. Savvy Gardening. https://savvygardening.com/kitchen-garden/

Browning, A. (2021, April 21). How to make Natural Dyes from Food (Step by step guide). FiberArtsy.Com; Annette Browning. https://www.fiberartsy.com/how-to-make-natural-dyes-from-food/

Carolynn. (2013, March 9). Survival candle-making 101. Off The Grid News. https://www.offthegridnews.com/current-events/top-headlines/survival-candle-making-101/

Esther. (2012, February 18). How to make your own soap. Off The Grid News. https://www.offthegridnews.com/current-events/top-headlines/how-to-make-your-own-soap/

Krane, J., & Bennett, J. (2018, November 6). 8 simple steps to arrange flowers like a pro. Better Homes & Gardens. https://www.bhg.com/decorating/home-accessories/flower-arranging/how-to-make-a-flower-arrangement/

May, R. (2014, September 12). How to make a quilt in six steps. Mother Earth News – The Original Guide To Living Wisely; Mother Earth News. https://www.motherearthnews.com/diy/how-to-make-a-quilt-ze0z1409zcwil